THE WARRIOR-PRIEST MINDSET

A Necessary Dichotomy for God's Chosen Knights

·Be ·Viligent
·

The Warrior-Priest Mindset: A Necessary Dichotomy for God's Chosen Knights
By Drew Graffia

Defender Publishing: Crane, MO 65633
©2020 by Thomas Horn, Defender Publishing. All rights reserved.
Published 2020
Printed in the United States of America

ISBN: 9781948014328

A CIP catalog record of this book is available from the Library of Congress.

Cover Illustration and Design by Jeffrey Mardis.

Unless otherwise noted, all Scripture from KJV

Unless otherwise noted, all Chapter Introductions are written by the author.

DEDICATION

To my Father in Heaven, you saved me from death and destruction and turned an evil man into a knight by showing me your love. For this I will always be in your service and you will always have my life as your own. I will never stop serving you. You are my King, my friend, and most of all you are my Father. I love you.

To my beautiful wife, Bri. I met you in a castle in California and took you on a wild, unpredictable, and shocking adventure to a faraway land. Thank you for trusting me to lead even when I barely know the way. You are my sacred gift from Heaven. You are my eyes when I am blind and you are my heart every single day. Everything about you is worth fighting for and that is exactly what I plan to do for the rest of our lives. I would marry you again and again if I could. I love you.

TABLE OF CONTENTS

THE LION AND THE LAMB

THE WARRIOR AND THE PRIEST

THE KNIGHT AND THE COUNTERFEIT CRUSADER

THE WARRIOR-PRIEST MINDSET

A Necessary Dichotomy for God's Chosen Knights

Learn the Gospel

That if thou shalt confess with thy mouth the Lord Jesus, and shalt believe in thine heart that God hath raised him from the dead, thou shalt be saved.
For with the heart man believeth unto righteousness; and with the mouth confession is made unto salvation.
Romans 10:9-10

Repent

From that time Jesus began to preach, and to say, Repent: for the kingdom of heaven is at hand.
Matthew 4:17

Follow the Warrior-Priest Code

Honour all men. Love the brotherhood. Fear God. Honour the king.
1 Peter 2:17

1.) You are responsible for
    Your walk with God.

    (Me)

2.) No One is going
    to remain viligent
    For you.

3.) It is a pleasure the
    to be given

    Honor
    to maintain and
    a sober
    viligent

INTRODUCTION:
THE BLACK AND
WHITE KNIGHT

Sweat drips down my face as I close the visor to my helmet. My vision narrows through the slits to where I can only see in front of me. It's probably for the best, so my focus can remain clear and my lance can strike true. My shield is clanging against my armor as my warhorse is becoming impatient...or scared. The roar of the crowd sometimes unsettles the young steed's nerves. This is all still new to him and his heart is racing. MY heart is racing as well but for a much different reason. Long gone are the days of apprehension and nervousness before battle. Now all that is left is the confident calm before the storm that experience brings. Make no mistake about it, the storm that follows the calm will be furious and unrelenting. Like a lion poised in place perfectly still until he explodes into a full-fledged war charge. Nothing will satisfy him except victory and nothing will stop him except death. Death… or the call of his King commanding him to show mercy.

Be viligent

• Stop & The Lord Help

The time has come and the trumpets are sounding. The Lord Chancellor starts announcing my entrance to the field of battle. "In prayer, he remains HUMBLE. In service, he is ever LOYAL. In battle, he is...INVINCIBLE!" My horse starts to trot in place and begins to tug on the reins. I feel the worn leather start to pull on my hand causing my shield to clink against my armor even more, making things worse on the poor horse's nerves. "Not yet, my friend, easy does it" I whisper. The last second before riding onto the field of battle can sometimes take an eternity to pass. Finally, the last words are spoken beckoning me out to do what I was trained for...what I was *made* for. "THE WARRIOR PRIEST. THE BLACK AND WHITE KNIGHT!" I storm the gates and make my way into the arena spurring my horse to a full canter as I make my triumphant entrance. I come to an abrupt halt upon reaching the center of the arena, slowing my horse to a stop as the rules of the joust are announced.

Some fight for glory...some fight for women...but I fight for my King. No amount of victory will ever be enough to honor Him. No amount of defeat will stop me from fighting. No speed of horse will outrun His protection. No battle wound can withstand His Holy Light. My eyes can see the arena filled with near 1300 screaming peasants and nobles but I know there are far greater legions of angels watching from beyond the stands. Watching...protecting.

My focus is crystal clear as I approach my foe. He fights for himself. I fight for my King. The only true loss I could experience would be failure to try my absolute best to bring honor and glory to my King through my deeds in the arena. Seems like I have the edge there. The Lord Chancellor's speech about the rules of the joust fades into the background as I begin to pray. "Father please protect us both. Believer and non-believer. Please forgive me for my sins and work through me tonight to bring honor to your name. Soothe the minds of these beasts we ride and keep the enemy from interfering in the tournament. Please let these people leave here with something special and let the children be inspired to follow your path for them. I love you Father, Amen."

I urge my horse to his starting point and raise my lance to signify that I am ready. Some say they are born ready. Not me. I worked for this. I went through the fire and trained for this. More often than not

I've even *failed* for this. The trumpets blare once again and the time for action is now! I charge forward watching my opponent grow larger as we approach. I lower the lance and hold my shield tight as I brace for impact. BOOM! Shards of wood explode all around us as my shoulder reels back in pain. He must have hit the sweet spot. It doesn't matter. "Arm another lance, make another pass!" the Lord Chancellor bellows. The next pass happens but this time I miss as his lance explodes once again against my shield sending me vaulting off of my horse into the sand below. When the blur of motion stops, I am on my back looking up at my squire who runs up to me with my weapons of warfare. He hands me my combat shield since my joust shield will no longer be needed. Then he hands me my sword. There is nothing in this world quite like a man holding a sword. Wielding it and feeling the endless possibilities for heroism...for justice...for honor. It instantly calls to mind the other sword that I wield that is not of this world and I utter another quick prayer.

It has all led up to this. The moment that separates the novice from the veteran. I look up to the dais and see the princess smiling at me. I will respect her and protect her at all costs but she is not to whom I bend my knee. I've seen far too many knights fall by the wayside and trade their righteous power for a strange woman's embrace. No. Not this knight. I stare at my earthly king and salute him. I know he will enjoy seeing his subjects battle. And I know my God-given skill will be a much-needed break in the monotony of other knights who have fought with the bare minimum of passion. Those who do not have the fire inside cannot be expected to light up the world. I know I have the fire inside. I feel it every day. Every waking moment urging me to push forward. There is always tomorrow. Defeat is for a day but to hear my King's approval lasts an eternity.

I smack my sword against my shield as a loud crash echoes through the arena followed by even louder cheers from the stands. I then salute my opponent. He does the same. Respect and honor. We are brothers. At different roads in life but brothers nonetheless. He had better be ready to leave it all on the battlefield because I will *never* let my fire be lessened to match that of the man across from me. The crowd is raging more than ever-thirsty for the war they came to see. We both charge in weapons swinging as the first strikes come together. I take the first hit on the shield and follow up with a shoulder strike of my own. He is faster than I thought. A flurry of swords sends sparks everywhere. Shards of metal shoot off of the swords and light up the arena. The crowd goes wild. I block a head strike and I dodge to the left. The sword narrowly misses me as I follow up with a waist cut backing him off. He sends strike after strike my way and my shield answers them all...all but the last one. I feel pain flood my body as blood drips from my forehead down into my eye.

"Do you need me to stop Sir Knight?" he asks me as we are locked weapon to weapon, vying for the upper hand. "NEVER!" I yell and I throw his sword up into the air and follow it with a kick to the back sending him sprawling across the sand. As I look up to the dais for one more salute, I see the look of concern on the king's face and the look of horror on the face of the princess. No time for this. I'll deal with it after. I jump into the air and fly down on him with a sword chop that would make any katana-wielding samurai jealous. I miss him by a hair's breadth as he rolls to the side. I notice his pace declining. "You're not done yet, are you?" I demand as he follows up with an equally bold reply of "You wish!" He follows up with his strongest strikes yet but I can still feel his pace declining. Now's my chance. I swing for the fences and smash the sword out of his hand exposing his soft underbelly. I see the wolf on his tunic and I know my shot is clear. SMACK!! I deliver the killing blow to his midsection as he slumps over and collapses to the ground.

I take a knee in the center of the arena with light shining all around me. I put my forehead on the pommel of my sword and thank my God that He got us through it. Fatigue finally hits me. Wiping blood out of my eye a smile hits my lips and I feel the pleasure of my True King wash over me as I do one of the things he specifically made me for. "You have fought valiantly and bravely WARRIOR-PRIEST! RISE AND HEAR THE CHEERS OF YOUR PEOPLE!" I stand and am showered with the roar of the crowd. I know the cheers are my Father's and I am just the earthly stand-in. I see lights and faces mixed together then my focus zeros in on a young boy smiling and waving intensely. I wave back and salute and he loses his mind with excitement then looks to his mom with wide eyes as I see him mouth "He waved at me, mommy!"

I had hoped to live out an honorable example of what a true knight is and seeing that boy's face reminds me of my true goal. There is a dichotomy in my very title and nature. I am the black and white knight. My King is the LION AND THE LAMB. I am... the WARRIOR-PRIEST!

The previous story was NOT metaphorical. It was NOT make-believe. It was a snapshot of my life from 2008-2018 when I worked as the Assistant Head Knight (actor/stuntman/instructor) at a popular medieval tournament dinner show (which I will refer to hereafter as "MT"). The job included weapon combat, jousting, horse-riding and training others to do the same. Since this book is not about me, I will spare you my complete autobiography. Though, to catch you up to speed, I'll share three points relevant to this work from my personal background:

⊕   I have always felt drawn towards all things knight-related.

⊕   As a young child, I can recall a deep desire to work at MT.

⊕   I became saved by The Lord in 2010.

The book you hold is a framework for living as a follower of the one true God, and His Son, King Jesus of Nazareth. Its purpose is twofold: to share what God has taught me and to share scriptures from my King which reinforce those teachings. The decade in which I found myself acting as a knight, most often *being* a knight, taught me that the traits of the stereotypical knight are in line with what God calls us to be.

I will go on record as saying I am in no way someone who has mastered everything in this book. I am a "knight in battered armor" who is fighting to follow the narrow and ancient path God has laid out for His chosen people. I often re-examine my steps, trying to follow His path, and trying to serve my God the way He wants us to serve Him. It is a never-ending journey where the ultimate reward is a relationship with Father as intended, walking hand in hand in the cool of the day through His glorious creation! Amen!

If you hear truth from this scroll then it is certainly the Father's wisdom at work. However, if you find any error, then it lies at the hands of this lowly servant who has undertaken the mission of expanding on God's truth the best way he could. Let the error be on my account and not on His!

When it comes to your walk with God, there is no preparatory period. At MT, when you are hired as a squire, you are in the show serving your knight day one! You are assisting in the fight day one. As someone holding this book, you are officially at the squire stage. You are to immediately begin your quest. But soon after, through hard work, dedication, obedience, and loyalty, you will be raised to the rank of Knight, fully ready to storm further into the fray and fight for your King!

It is my prayer that this book will *convict* you in areas of your life where you have yielded ground to your enemies. I pray these written words will destroy any feeble excuses that stand between you and obedience to your Perfect King. Lastly, I pray that these pages will *motivate* you to take up the Sword of the Spirit to STAND AND FIGHT! Done are the days of complacency. This isn't someone else's sin. This isn't information that will be the next new thing to be learned and forgotten soon after. This is your walk from here forward, your sin, and your responsibility to be a "DOER of the word and not just a HEARER (James 1:22)".

WHY AN⊕+HER B⊕⊕K?

Let us start off by answering a very important question: why another book? Well since you wish to be so forward, I'll tell you! The Bible is the ultimate knight's tale ever told and many people fail to even notice it! Don't believe me? Let's take a look!

The Great King Yahweh has peace throughout His realm until an ancient and evil dragon terrorizes the King's people and deceives them into giving up their membership status in His divine council and inhabitants of the royal garden. As a consequence, for his deception, the King banishes the great dragon but not before giving a prophecy telling one day a noble knight would be born that would remove the curse from upon God's people. He would be struck in the heel by the ancient dragon but He would then crush the head of the foul beast. Centuries later the realm is a mess and when all hope seems lost the humble knight disguised as a peasant shows up to lift the curse. Once it is revealed He is the son of the King, He is taken captive by the minions of the dragon, tortured, and sentenced to death on a cross. The King's people and the dragon included think that the prophecy has failed as their Knight hangs dead on a tree until by the greatest miracle of all, He rises from the dead! He had fooled the dragon into capturing Him, thereby succeeding in lifting the curse! It was revealed that because of His righteousness, the King gave Him power over death and He was able to come back to life and restore humanity to their former state as members His divine council and inhabitants of the royal garden. However, the dragon was weakened yet not defeated and continued to terrorize the King's people as the knight headed home to His Father the King. Before He left, the noble knight said that one day He would return. Not as a peasant but instead in His true knightly glory, riding through the clouds on His white war horse with legions of His Holy Ones, ready to face the dragon one last time. He will slay all the minions of the dragon and then finally chop the head off of that ancient beast. After He chains the dragon's body up in the darkest dungeon, He will finally claim His bride, Lady Church, and returns to His Father's kingdom to live in peace for all eternity! There is no better story than this!

A TIME FOR WAR

It goes without saying that in these last days there has been a full-blown attack on biblical manhood and biblical femininity. Transgenderism, drag queen predators teaching children in libraries, homosexuality on parade, third trimester and partial birth abortion are all part of everyday life. Mark my words, up next we will see the normalization and acceptance of pedophilia and cannibalism, which is disgusting and sad. We truly live in a barbaric time once again.

The enemy has not only assaulted our castle but is now desecrating our Great Hall as we sit and watch these foul knaves trample underfoot all that is Holy. God does not overlook these things and He is "not slack concerning his promise, as some men count slackness; but is longsuffering to us-ward, not willing that any should perish, but that all should come to repentance" (2 Peter 3:9). He knows the perfect time for the counter-attack. It grieves my heart to think of what God feels as He looks at our nation. Our nation is a dwelling place for demons and it is high time for God's chosen class of elite warriors to rise up from the wastes and join the war raging around them.

You have been summoned to the battlefield and whether you want to fight or not, you are still enlisted! Every warrior has a role to play and an impact to make and if you shrink away from your duty then you are not worthy of the reward. This does not mean that your works earn your salvation but rather works are expected from every true believer as a sign of their faith.

> But someone will say, "You have faith, and I have works." Show me your faith without your works, and I will show you my faith by my works. You believe that there is one God. You do well. Even the demons believe—and tremble! But do you want to know, O foolish man, that faith without works is dead? - James 2:18-20

Many people will depend on you in this life and you are not to let them down by lying idle on the sidelines while the battle rages on around you. Even your King joins the fray and fights alongside you so what is your excuse? You have none. He will empower you in this war and teach you how to fight. He clears your path with His left hand while holding you up with his right. The odds are in your favor, fellow warrior.

He teacheth my hands to war, so that a bow of steel
is broken by mine arms. Thou hast also given me the
shield of thy salvation: and thy right hand hath holden
me up, and thy gentleness hath made me great. Thou
hast enlarged my steps under me, that my feet did not
slip. - Psalms 18 34:36

If the war hasn't affected those in your camp yet then you are either
blind or about to have your world rocked. Either way, you need to be
prepared, spiritually more than anything else. You can store up all the
food you want but if you aren't hearing from the Most High then you
might as well hand over your goods to the brigands or highwaymen
that come to loot and kill the ones you love. There is a time for peace
and a time for war and I believe for the sect of God's Warrior-Priests,
it is a TIME FOR WAR! War on sin, war on the flesh, and war on all
the evil that threatens our women and children seeking to herd us
all like cattle into their pens like cattle for the slaughter. As Solomon
explains in Ecclesiastes 3:8 "[There is] A time to love, and a time to
hate; a time of war, and a time of peace."

A time to love, and a time to hate; a time of war, and a
time of peace - Ecclesiastes 3:8

Practice makes perfect and you can't expect God to let you chop off the
head of a Nephilim warrior if you can't even control your temper. There
will be a time where you are capable of amazing feats by the power of
God but in order to get there, you have to start where you are. You must
conquer the smaller battles before you can win the war. You need to
develop the muscle memory for war, which comes from winning small
battles day by day. It is through discipline and commitment to your faith
that you will become stronger in The Lord. Your King will train you to
fight and even fight *with* you so long as you are in right-standing with
Him. He will lead you to do *His* will and *His* good pleasure.

He that is faithful in that which is least is faithful also in much: and he that is unjust in the least is unjust also in much. - Luke 16:10

For it is God which worketh in you both to will and to do of his good pleasure. - Philippians 2:13

The great warrior Caleb recalling his journey to spy out the Promised Land God vowed to deliver into his people's hands said something inspiring and empowering. He said, "I am still as strong today as I was in the day that Moses sent me!" Did you get that? He was as strong at eighty-five as he was at forty! Father God kept him youthful and strong in order to do his work and conquer the Promised Land!

And now, behold, the Lord has kept me alive, just as he said, these forty-five years since the time that the Lord spoke this word to Moses, while Israel walked in the wilderness. And now, behold, I am this day eighty-five years old. I am still as strong today as I was in the day that Moses sent me; my strength now is as my strength was then, for war and for going and coming. - Joshua 14:11 ESV

If you walk the righteous path and diligently seek to know the face of your Father, then you will get to experience God's supernatural hedge of protection around you while you continue in the quest that He has called you to. He will give you the strength and endurance to never surrender. When you see this journey through till the end, you will enter into eternity ready to kneel before the throne and hear those fateful words..."Well done, good and faithful servant".

THE JOURNEY BEGINS: BROTHERS IN ARMS

To begin your training, we must meet those who will fight by your side. Remember, more blades make light work of your foes! Your enemy fights dirty and has no qualms about cheating. There are no lines the enemy won't cross. Nothing is sacred to this horde of mangy curs. You will need all the help you can get and having *faithful* and *trustworthy* brothers by your side is a major advantage. If you have unreliable friends who care more about telling you their victories than they do about celebrating in yours, then you are in a dire situation. If your friends do not console you in times of pain but instead treat you like Job's friends treated him, then you have bad friends! It is better to have NO friends than bad friends.

Some life changing advice I have heard on my quest was when I heard a man say "I prayed for God to remove friends from my life who He doesn't want me to have and bring friends into my life that He wants for me. I want HIM to choose not me." (Paraphrasing). I highly recommend you pray this prayer as I also have. Never forget, iron sharpens iron and there are friends that stick closer than a brother. This is not merely a "Christianese" saying to make you feel warm inside. It is a tried and true battle truth. You need to hone your craft and prepare your weapons for war. Just as a sword is sharpened for the day of battle, you will be sharpened by other believers. It is a strong and meaningful concept that should not be viewed lightly.

> Iron sharpeneth iron; so a man sharpeneth the countenance of his friend. - Proverbs 27:17

> A man that hath friends must shew himself friendly: and there is a friend that sticketh closer than a brother. - Proverbs 18:24

In order to have good friends, you must also BE a good friend. When you talk to others don't let everything that comes out of your mouth be about *your* life and *your* aspirations. Ask people about what's going on with them. This is a great way to start replacing pride with humility. Be slow to speak and quick to listen. Go above and beyond for your friends all the while realizing that people aren't perfect. You know very well about all of your own shortcomings. Having an impossibly high standard of friendship for others that you yourself could not even bear is unwise and graceless, to say the least. We must have *grace* for others and more importantly learn to *forgive*. We will delve deeper into forgiveness in a later chapter.

Allow me to describe a scenario for you to better explain what I am trying to convey. Picture a man riding in a heavy cart filled with goods from the merchants in town. It is being pulled by an old sway-backed Palomino who is at the end of its days. The old Palomino breathed its last breath and falls over dead. The man is completely distraught for he had this horse ever since he was but a small child. Not only did he lose a friend but also a great worker and a huge part of his livelihood. As he is pulling his cart by hand to the side of the road, he starts to sweat from the hot summer sun beating down on his brow. He sees his friend in the distance who also has a small bag of goods, running to meet him. "I saw that your horse had fallen and although I may be late for supper, I shall set my goods in your cart and carry one side whilst you carry the other! For I am greatly sorry that you lost such a great beast and I know how dear the old steed was to your heart. Let us take your cart to my home and I shall lend you my draft horse to pull it the rest of the way to your home. Surely you can keep the steed until you replace the one you lost. Here, drink from my water satchel and let us make way to my cottage. Before we go, we shall pray together beseeching The Lord to bring some peace into such a poor turn of events and protect us on our way."

Try to imagine what the man was feeling when he saw his friend running up to help him. If he wasn't already tearing up from losing his horse, he might have teared up right then from the great relief his companion brought to him. When the friend then sacrificed his plans and offered to help carry the tremendously heavy cart without being asked, it is safe to assume that the man felt immense gratitude to have such a selfless and true friend. Not only did the friend alter his own plans for a friend in need but the task he agreed to help was not an easy one! Carrying a heavy cart through the hot sun was no minor feat. The friend then *consoled* his weary brother and offered him water and *prayer*.

How many of your friends would do this? Or when you call them to help you move to a new house, do they make excuses? And if they do help, is it with a distracted or upset attitude? They simply cannot be bothered to lift a finger without an adequate reward. People even unknowingly put their own busy schedule of social media and television as excuses not to help as they bow down to worship the "Sloth god of Laziness." Are *you* the one that is slow to help your friends or has a bad attitude while doing so? I wager at times we all have been. The goal is to never be this kind of companion, for we know that our Savior, Yeshua, was nothing like these fair-weather friends. He gave us a selfless and loving example of how to treat others. He also showed us the great capacity to forgive that He expects in every one of us.

Life casts heavy and unexpected burdens on us all and Jesus asks us to cast our burdens on Him. He also commands us to carry each other's burdens to lighten the load that this world encumbers us with. Jesus told us that the key to greatness is through servitude to others. Let us not balk away from such acts of service to others.

Cast thy burden upon the Lord, and he shall sustain thee: he shall never suffer the righteous to be moved. - Psalm 55:22

Bear ye one another's burdens, and so fulfill the law of Christ. - Galatians 6:2

But he that is greatest among you shall be your servant. - Matthew 23:11

That being said, if you have a friend who helps carry your burden but complains the whole time or seems sorely vexed, they had to be inconvenienced to help you, then it is better to have no help at all. A friend that brings you down and acts in a way that is contrary to your life as a believer is like a thorn in your boot. It is better to have no friends than to have bad friends. The last thing you want is an enemy in your camp. This life can become very lonely at times and there may be seasons where you seemingly have no friends at all but do not lose heart! Keep praying and asking Father to provide you with the friends He has chosen for you while removing those He has not. We are sometimes called to walk alone for seasons of our life but always remember, the believer is *never* truly alone because he has his most faithful friend, the God of the Holy Scriptures.

I've said it before and I'll say it again, it is easier to be brought down than it is to be brought up. An anchor would have no trouble sinking you to the bottom of the depths but if you tried to bring that same anchor up to the water's surface then you would have a near-impossible task ahead of you. Here's some free advice...get rid of the anchors! You become like the people you surround yourself with (Proverbs 13:20) and there is no fellowship between light and darkness (Ephesians 5:11). Time is short and your days are numbered (Ephesians 5:16), so spend your time with people that edify, motivate, teach, and look out for you.

CHAPTER I
HOW THE KING
VIEWS HIS KNIGHTS

What was I thinking!? I look back at my arrogance in disgust for asking father to give me my inheritance before his time. How disrespectful and blind I have become. Wasting my father's gift on women and drink. How was I to know the famine was to come? Everyone is starving and destitute in the streets and I am no different. Sleeping in the fields with the swine, fighting for their scraps!

Surely, I can convince the old man to take me back as a servant. Even they are treated better than this. I'll plead my case and he will have no choice other than to take me back...hopefully. Lord knows I do not deserve it. I am utterly worthless and a complete failure so why not make my shame complete and run home with my tail between my legs? There he is just over the hill. I have my speech prepared and I will beg if I have to...what is left of my pride anyway?

"Son! SON!" Father shouted as he ran to meet the young man.

Is he running to me? Maybe his anger has been stirred up farther than I thought. Too late to go back now though, I thought in my head.

"Son, OH how I have missed you so badly. I feared I would never see you again. Finally, my tears will cease to flow!" said the old man as he embraced his son with the strength of many bears and kissed his cheek.

"I am not worthy of this father! I have betrayed you and the God we serve to be received with open arms?! I do not deserve this." the young man cried as he fell to the floor in utter disbelief.

"Zerek" the father replied "Grab my purple robe and the shoes by the bed! Dempha! Grab the fatted calf in the main stall! Tonight, we shall celebrate! For today is the day my son has returned, and with him so does my happiness!"

In order to build a strong castle, you must first build an even stronger foundation. In order to sift through the lies of the enemy, you must first know the truth of your Liege, Lord Yahweh. What is that truth? Your awakening started when Your King saw the scroll of your misdeeds in this life. Upon the giving of your confession, followed by your plea for mercy, He heard you. Like the father of the prodigal son, upon your return, He runs to meet you with open arms, for He knows your true value. He sacrificed the life of His own son to stay the blade of the executioner and spare you the death sentence your wretched sin has earned you. He re-forged you like a blacksmith removing the imperfections from the weapon's metal through the fire and flames. You were destroyed so you could be remade into your true form as His imager. Once His image in was refined, He then grafted you into His family tree. He made you a joint heir with His son who conquered the grave. Now an heir to the throne of the Ancient of Days, you are given your mission.

> My people are destroyed for lack of knowledge: because thou hast rejected knowledge, I will also reject thee, that thou shalt be no priest to me: seeing thou hast forgotten the law of thy God, I will also forget thy children. - Hosea 4:6

Without *truth,* we let *fear* reign in our minds and lives. His Lordship says that people are destroyed for lack of knowledge. What knowledge? Knowledge of his royal commandments and laws. Without knowing what He says is true about you and without knowing the laws of His kingdom, we are left destitute and alone in facing life's trials. If someone told you that at first light tomorrow you were to be executed, chances are your mind would run wild with fear. Now let's say you knew the deliverer of that bad news was actually one of the townsfolk playing a prank on you. You're worry would then turn to relief. To know the counterfeit, you must first master the truth. Knowing the truth about the situation would likely eliminate your fear. The more familiar we are with King Yahweh's scriptures, the more the enemy's lies will stand out like a sore thumb.

He teaches you His ways and gives you your new heavenly armor to withstand supernatural attack as well as physical. As He hands you your shield, you realize the family crest on the shield is that of your Protector and Teacher. Lastly, He gives you the sword, blazing brighter than the sun and sharpened on both sides. IT IS TIME TO FIGHT!

You aren't sent to the front lines just yet but you are taken to the battlefield. Your mission is clear and your enemies are described to you. Sin is their method of invasion and you then realize that you have its dark tendrils wrapped around your life in various different areas. Sin will attempt to trick you into caring for it and nursing it as your own private pet. You are fooled into protecting it for fear of discomfort or the loss of a pleasure. First, you must destroy the enemy closest to you. If you think that you will be able to destroy the dragons that lie ahead yet you cannot even keep peace with your fellow knights right beside you, then you are gravely mistaken.

The battles start small. If you want to be a great man of God but you are doing drugs or looking at pornography, how far do you think your Holy King will take you before you are confronted by Him? *Struggling* with sin implies a fight but being accepting of your sin is a self-imposed death sentence. Never forget that you represent your King and you are called to destroy the unfruitful works of darkness, not be a part of them. Again, you are not just called to "disagree" with darkness but rather to *destroy* it!

This will alienate you from your fellow countrymen and often times leave you alone in your stand for righteousness. You must then ask yourself "What is of more value? The acceptance of my earthly peers or the acceptance of my Heavenly Father?" You might as well ask, "What is of more value; sleeping in a barn with pigs or sleeping in a comfortable bed?" The questions are the same. If you wear King Jesus' crest on your shield and commit sinful deeds while doing so, do you think you will go unpunished? It is a *loving* father who cares enough to discipline his child when they go astray as opposed to letting them drift away in their own folly.

Once you repent of your sins and genuinely ask for forgiveness the charges against you are dropped. Without repentance, you are not acknowledging your sin and owning up to it so the charges against you will not be dropped. After repenting you now can wear *His* righteousness and continue on trying to not sin (obeying His laws) while repenting if you do. If He doesn't keep track of your sins once He removes them then why would you think you can? You are not to be a self-accusing and guilt-ridden soldier. You are to take the grace He lovingly gives and do something with it. Do not take this lightly! The grace of God is not a provision for sin! (Romans 13:14). It is an outstretched hand from the Father to pull you out of the ditches of trouble you fall into from being in your frail human form. This does not mean you can intentionally jump into trouble and take the hand of your Father for granted! To repent means to walk the other way. Go, and sin no more (John 8:11)

You are to *obey*. You are to be ready to *fight* for His Kingdom at any time and in whatever way He commands. You serve Him by His means, not by your own. You are not the one who gets to decide the terms of your relationship with your King. Much like in the medieval era, what the king says goes. He defines the terms of His kingdom. He makes it very clear what sin, obedience, and worship are. He also makes it clear who His children are. Never think that *you* are the one who gets to set the parameters of these things. King Yahweh is a discerner of the thoughts and intents of the heart (Jeremiah 17:10) and nothing can be hidden from He who sees all. It is time we all put *His* knowledge above *our* emotions. If you love The King you will obey His commandments and if you obey His commandments you will receive the great reward of an eternity in the Kingdom of the Father!

I want to be clear about something. We are all valuable to God but He does not *need* any one of us. He is the Alpha and Omega, the creator of the universe, and fully complete as is. He lacks nothing. He *chose* to love us. He *chose* to redeem us. Let us not make the mistake of overstating our value. He did not have to die because of how valuable we are but instead chose to die to save us from how depraved we had become. We did not earn His love but instead earned His wrath! Yet, He is so gracious to us and instead of giving us what we deserved, He gave us mercy. We are indeed valuable but we are not something that He was lacking, which makes it even more awesome that He chose to let us be a part of the picture!

If ye love me, keep my commandments (John 14:15)

In summary, let's see how our King views us:

⊕ **Valuable and worth saving** - The very fact that Jesus died for us shows we have value to Him and His plans for us. He does not get bored and does not do things without a purpose. He reconciled us for a reason. He is a God of order not of randomness or chaos.

Are not two sparrows sold for a farthing? and one of them shall not fall on the ground without your Father. But the very hairs of your head are all numbered. Fear ye not therefore, ye are of more value than many sparrows. -Matthew 10:29-31

What man of you, having an hundred sheep, if he lose one of them, doth not leave the ninety and nine in the wilderness, and go after that which is lost, until he find it? And when he hath found it, he layeth it on his shoulders, rejoicing. And when he cometh home, he calleth together his friends and neighbours, saying unto them, rejoice with me; for I have found my sheep which was lost. - Luke 15:4-6

⊕ **Given a purpose and a quest to complete** - Again we see that Yahweh is not a God of randomness but a God of order who does things purposefully and planned out from the beginning of time.

For we are his workmanship, created in Christ Jesus unto good works, which God hath before ordained that we should walk in them. - Ephesians 2:10

⊕ **Fearfully and wonderfully made by hand and breathed into by Yahweh Himself** - We are not carelessly or haphazardly created but rather carefully and beautifully made. God breathed His own breath into us and made us in His own image.

I will praise thee; for I am fearfully and wonderfully made: marvelous are thy works; and that my soul knoweth right well. - Psalms 139:14

And the Lord God formed man of the dust of the ground, and breathed into his nostrils the breath of life; and man became a living soul. - Genesis 2:7

⊕ **Cleansed of your past and given new grace each passing day** - When we confess our sins our King is quick to forgive us and wipe our slate clean, so to speak. He does not hold our past crimes against us once we are truly repentant and begin to seek after His ways.

If we confess our sins, he is faithful and just to forgive us our sins, and to cleanse us from all unrighteousness. - 1 John 1:9

⊕ **Restored and recreated upon entering His kingdom** - Once you are enlisted in His royal Kingdom, you are given a new life and a new beginning. The sins you sought after no longer have the power to bind you and you are set free from your crimes done in ignorance. Free to start anew.

Therefore, if any man be in Christ, he is a new creature: old things are passed away; behold, all things are become new. - 2 Corinthians 5:17

⊕ **Subject to His kingdom on His terms** - We are all under His command and His authority. The creator is always greater than the one created. It is by His will we were even called into existence.

Submit yourselves therefore to God. Resist the devil, and he will flee from you. - James 4:7

⊕ **Called to be OBEDIENT** - A King expects obedience from His people as a good father expects obedience from his children.

And it shall come to pass, if thou shalt hearken diligently unto the voice of the Lord thy God, to observe and to do all his commandments which I command thee this day, that the Lord thy God will set thee on high above all nations of the earth: - Deuteronomy 28:1

⊕ **Called to be HOLY** - We are made in the King's image to walk out His will. He is holy; therefore, we must also strive to be holy like the one whose image we bear.

But as he which hath called you is holy, so be ye holy in all manner of conversation; Because it is written, Be ye holy; for I am holy. And if ye call on the Father, who without respect of persons judgeth according to every man's work, pass the time of your sojourning here in fear - 1 Peter 1:15-17

⊕ **A warring knight who should be ready to fight evil at any moment** - We are in a spiritual battle from the moment we are born. The forces of darkness are always seeking to devour those made in the King's image. We must always be ready to fight in service to our King. While we will fight many physical battles, we must always remember our true battle is spiritual.

And have no fellowship with the unfruitful works of darkness, but rather reprove them. - Ephesians 5:11

For we wrestle not against flesh and blood, but against principalities, against powers, against the rulers of the darkness of this world, against spiritual wickedness in high places. - Ephesians 6:12

⊕ **We are priests whose focus lies more in God's eternal heavenly realm than the goings-on of our temporal earthly realm** - Although we live in the physical realm, for the time being, we are not focused solely on the cares of this world. We are priests who focus more on spiritual growth than physical gain.

Set your affection on things above, not on things on the earth. - Colossians 3:2

Lay not up for yourselves treasures upon earth, where moth and rust doth corrupt, and where thieves break through and steal: But lay up for yourselves treasures in heaven, where neither moth nor rust doth corrupt, and where thieves do not break through nor steal - Matthew 6:19-20

You have a *purpose* in life and were put here to do the good works He ordained for you to do (Ephesians 2:10)! You are a relentless HOLY WARRIOR who makes war for the expansion of your King's realm in a dark and twisted land. You are a **WARRIOR-PRIEST**! Now I believe it is time we uncover your first piece of armor...the Helmet of Salvation.

HELMET OF SALVATION

And take the helmet of salvation... - Ephesians 6:17

As with any proper knight in service to a king, you will need armor with which to protect you while you make war on the enemy. Our King has blessed everyone in His service with a full set of armor including a shield and a sword (Ephesians 6:10-18). The first piece that you have discovered through our journey together in search of the Warrior-Priest Mindset, is the Helmet of Salvation. It is a fully covered helmet including protection for the neck and the sides of the face. In the physical realm, this helmet will protect your head; however, in the spiritual realm it protects your thoughts and identity. The enemy forces will be mounting attacks in both realms from their location in the spiritual realm and you will need this vital piece of armor to deflect their attempts on your life.

This helmet provides the best truthful view on what our King has done for us through salvation and the truth about why He did it. It makes your mind impervious to the enemy's lies because it guards against them with the truth, which is the word of God. Romans 12:2 tells us to be transformed by the renewing of our mind. The Greek word for mind is "*nous*" and can be understood as mind, reason or understanding. The way I like to refer to it is *perspective*.

> **Perspective** (noun) - a particular attitude toward or way of regarding something; a point of view.

Perspective is summed up easily as the way you choose to view things. If your perspective is based on the lies that the enemy tells you about you being weak, worthless, unlovable, and unwanted then you will be completely manipulated by the enemy forces and never able to achieve your full effectiveness and potential as a knight in Yahweh's army. Like a knight with armor that is too heavy for him, you will be weighed down and unfit to fight. David himself refused to wear King Saul's armor when he fought Goliath of Gath because it was too heavy and would impede his ability to move. Instead of carrying the extra weight of the enemy's lies we must have a perspective that is drawn from the truths in the Word of God. You will find that when you know the truth and are familiar with it, the fiery lies that are presented before you look like cheap counterfeits and easily bounce off of your Helmet of Salvation.

> And be not conformed to this world: but be ye transformed by the renewing of your mind, that ye may prove what is that good, and acceptable, and perfect, will of God. - Romans 12:2

The enemies of our Kingdom and their dark commander will stop at nothing to rob you of any peace and joy. They wish to render us ineffective, powerless, and useless for the kingdom. They wish to replace our beautiful identity in Christ Jesus with a deadly fake that leads us astray into anger and bitterness. If they can get us to reject ourselves, others or God then they win. We will not let this happen, soldiers! The enemy tells us we are worthless but God tells us we were "fearfully and wonderfully made" (Psalm 139:14). The enemy tells us we have no purpose yet Yahweh tells us we are "predestined to be adopted as His sons through Jesus Christ" (Ephesians 1:5). We are adopted into the family of God thereby severing our connection to our previous family of darkness and freeing us from any debts we owed them. He clears our account and provides a new life with a valuable purpose. We know that there is nothing at all that we can do to earn the salvation that is a gift freely given by the Father (Ephesians 1:6). He provided this for us not because we are so valuable (though we do have value to Him) but because of *who He is*. He is a savior. He is a loving Father. He saved us without an ounce of work on our part. The enemy tries to get you to earn God's love in which we all fall short. The enemy tries to hold our past sins and past life against us but we know our Father has offered us every lasting forgiveness if we only repent and ask it of Him. The Holy Spirit decided that He is the seal on the scroll of our lives (Ephesians 1:13) and just like a scroll from medieval times, the seal represents protection, ownership, and authenticity. We are owned by God and under His protective wings.

Even the most powerful of all fallen angels, demons, or anything else must submit to our King Jesus and to His name used by His people. He is "far above all principality, and power, and might, and dominion, and every name that is named, not only in this world but also in that which is to come" (Ephesians 1:21) as any rightful and sovereign King should be. We are called to reject the lies of the enemy and instead recite the truths of God in their place. I make it a habit to pray whenever an inappropriate or mean thought comes into my head. It sounds something like:

> "Father God I rebuke those thoughts in your name and give them over to you. I thank you that I am no longer that person and ask that you clear these from my mind and fill them with your peace and love, amen".

We are to take every thought captive (2 Corinthians 10:5) and throw out the evil while keeping the righteous. To take a thought captive does not mean to politely ask it to leave but rather to grab it by the back of the neck and throw it out the doors of your mind while thanking God for the authority to do so!

Our confidence and strength come from the word of God and it is the source from which we draw our identity. Strengthen your mind with these truths and fill your head with scripture and prayer every day. By doing so you are forging your Helmet of Salvation into a stronger piece of armor, upgrading its quality with every passing moment. Memorize verses as you would memorize battle strategies. Walk righteously and accept what God freely offers while you equip your beautiful Helmet of Salvation!

Now you must equip your new helmet and we dive into deeper waters. Measure everything that you read in this scroll against the Word of God. Do not leave it up to me to teach you but rather prove yourself a worthy student who refuses to take anyone's word for what The Bible says without first fact-checking it themselves. That being said, let us now dig into one of the major themes of this tale...dichotomies.

CHAPTER 2
THE SUFFERING SERVANT AND THE CONQUERING KING

He was oppressed and He was afflicted,
Yet He did not open His mouth;
Like a lamb that is led to slaughter,
And like a sheep that is silent before its shearers,
So He did not open His mouth. – Isaiah 53:7

And then shall appear the sign of the Son of man in heaven: and then shall
all the tribes of the earth mourn, and they shall see the Son of man coming
in the clouds of heaven with power and great glory. – Matthew 24:30

DICHOTOMY DEFINED

When thinking of a knight, it is near impossible not to also think of his moral code of chivalry or his heroic deeds of righteousness. A knight without those things wouldn't really be that great of a knight, right? When we think "knight" most of us picture a holy warrior who is kneeling in prayer with his hands on a sword. That's what's in your mind, right? Good, because that's what we're talking about. What we are not talking about are the knights from the Crusades, knights of Freemasonry, or the Knights Templar. Those are orders with dark roots in Gnosticism, the Vatican, and the occult. A lot of their costumes have black, white, and red, similar to the "black and white knight" archetype we are using for this book. However, the reason I chose our specific "black and white knight" archetype is that more often than not I played the role of this knight during my time at the medieval dinner tournament I worked at. The version of the knight I portrayed was a warrior-priest who fought for his God and fought with honor. It is a far cry from the Templars, Crusaders, or Freemasons.

For the purposes of the book, I wish to divorce any connection from *our* "black and white knight" to any of those factions. Sure, there are bad knights but that doesn't characterize the whole group. However, the good traits of the knight archetype tend to do that very thing. With this, we will form our new knight with his core ideals rooted in scripture and examine the dichotomies that are ever-present in his existence. What is a dichotomy, you ask?

> **Dichotomy** - a division or contrast between two things that are or are represented as being opposed or entirely different.

Here are the examples we are working with. On my battle tunic at work, I had black stripes and white stripes. If either of those components were removed then I would not have that same tunic. It would then be something different. Black and white are almost as opposite as it gets yet they both were needed to make that specific tunic.

To start off we will examine the dichotomy I like to refer to as "The Suffering Servant and the Conquering King" dichotomy. This is in reference to How Jesus was viewed during His first coming and how He is prophesied to be during His second coming. Then I am going to lay out two dichotomies that are intrinsically built into every warrior of God and even in the Son of Man himself. The first of those we will get into the will be the "Lion and the Lamb" dichotomy. We will then examine the second: "The Warrior and the Priest". After exploring each side of both dichotomies, we will then move onto the combination of all four terms...the KNIGHT. Now that you are privy to the battle plan, let us continue on our journey!

THE TWO MESSIAHS?

To start off our adventure we uncover one of the most fascinating dichotomies found within Yeshua's Kingdom. The "Two Messiahs" dichotomy or as I call it "The Suffering Servant and the Conquering King." Never heard? Well then, let us unpack this concept and travel deeper into the rich mysteries of our Savior King.

First-century Jews had a long history of pain and unhappiness by the time Jesus had arrived. They had already been under heavy oppression and were exiled by the Babylonians, governed and ruled over by the Persians and conquered by the Romans. They hung on for dear life to the fact that they were promised a savior to rescue them from the evil hands of their captors. They were promised a "*Mashiach*" the Hebrew word for Messiah.

The Jewish people heard tales of a coming "Conquering King" who would save them from the terrors they were plagued with. He would arrive "triumphantly in the clouds" (Daniel 7:13) to bring swift and righteous judgment to the unjust and restore the Kingdom of God back to His chosen people. A valiant hero that would step foot onto the field of battle with legions of warring angels ready to set fire to the wicked before sitting upon His glorious throne (Matt 25:31). They would finally be delivered from exile while their Conquering King would lay waste to their enemies and bring about the Messianic Era of peace, also known as the Millennial Reign.

> ...and they shall beat their swords into plowshares, and
> their spears into pruning hooks: nation shall not lift up
> sword against nation, neither shall they learn war any
> more. - Isaiah 2:4

ᛗESSIAH BEN DAVID

They called their hero Messiah ben David because He would come from the bloodline of King David. Not only that but He would have many similarities to King David himself beyond just His lineage. In our modern times, we have the benefit of a complete, bound Bible available to us and we can easily identify their prophesied Messiah ben David as our Lord Jesus, while the people of antiquity did not have this luxury. Knowing this we can examine several ways that He was similar to King David. We know from 1 Samuel 17 that David was a shepherd who by the age of fourteen had already slain a lion and a bear that had tried to attack one of the sheep in his care. David himself referred to our Lord as his shepherd (Psalm 23:1). Lord Jesus was described as "that great shepherd of the sheep" (Hebrews 13:20) and also the shepherd of our souls (1 Peter 2:25). A shepherd was called to protect and watch over his sheep. They would sometimes even leave the ninety-nine sheep to chase after the one that got away (Luke 15:3-7). When the tribes of Israel gathered around David at Mt. Hebron, they reminded him that The Lord charged him with this statement: "Thou shalt feed my people Israel, and thou shalt be a captain over Israel." (2 Samuel 5:2). In the same way that David was to protect his sheep and risked his life for them, Lord Jesus would protect His sheep and even GIVE His life for them. King David and Lord Jesus surprisingly both exhibited the "Lamb" side of the Lion/Lamb Dichotomy through being good shepherds AND the "Lion" side by being ferocious warriors.

The correlations do not stop there. David and Jesus were anointed kings chosen personally by Yahweh. David ruled over Israel after King Saul was slain and the kingdom was specifically given to him by God through the prophet Samuel. Samuel was told by Yahweh to keep searching through the sons of Jesse until he finally landed on David (1 Samuel 16:8-12). After Saul disobeyed God and had his kingship removed, Samuel told him that his kingdom was given to one who was better than he (1 Samuel 15:28). Yeshua was also chosen by Yahweh to be the King of Kings and Lord of Lords. (Revelation 19:16). He was "the Word made flesh" that "dwelt among us, and "we beheld his glory, the glory as of the only begotten of the Father, full of grace and truth" (John 1:14).

David and Yeshua were both great heroes that saved their people from destruction in times of need. David was the only man brave enough to take on that blasphemous Philistine, Goliath, and he was only fourteen! With one shot from his sling and one cut from that unholy Nephilim's own blade, he was able to rescue his people from war and save many lives. When we look at Jesus, we see that He, too, was a great hero who with one sacrifice was able to cut the legs off of that old crusty serpent and save humanity from the clutches of death and slavery. When He actually returns as Messiah ben David, He will then finish the job and eventually cut the HEAD off of that foul beast and imprison him for all eternity. Hallelujah, or as my knightly brethren say HUZZAH!

> "And David my servant shall be king over them; and they all shall have one shepherd: they shall also walk in my judgments, and observe my statutes, and do them."
> - Ezekiel 37:24

> When the Son of man shall come in his glory, and all the holy angels with him, then shall he sit upon the throne of his glory: And before him shall be gathered all nations: and he shall separate them one from another, as a shepherd divideth his sheep from the goats: And he shall set the sheep on his right hand, but the goats on the left. - Matthew 25:31-33

For the Israelites awaiting their savior, this was all fine and good except for one minor detail - there were many other prophecies that described a messiah that was the exact *opposite*. What were they to do with a myriad of verses that were seemingly in contradiction to their Warrior Messiah? The same Holy Scriptures where they learned about the Conquering King also has mention of a far more peculiar messiah alongside them. The Suffering Servant.

The prophecies spoke of a Suffering Servant that would come to His people riding on a lowly donkey (Zechariah 9:9) as humble as you please. Zechariah 12:10 prophesied people would "mourn for him, as one mourneth for his only son, and shall be in bitterness for him, as one that is in bitterness for his firstborn." Moreover, the death of this Suffering Servant would be followed by great calamities and even *more* tribulations for Israel (Obadiah 1:18)! This was a stark contrast to the crowned Valiant Knight in the bloody robes that would storm to Earth on a white war horse with His eyes a flame of fire and set the house of Esau (Edom) ablaze with armies of soldiers trailing behind Him (Revelation 19:11-14). Instead, this Priest Messiah would come to atone for the sins of Israel and go like a sheep to the slaughter silently into His executioner's hands. He was the Suffering Servant who was also referred to as another name...the Messiah Ben Joseph.

MESSIAH BEN JOSEPH

This Messiah ben Joseph character was descended from the line of Joseph, son of Jacob and Rachel. He was called the Suffering Servant because Joseph was also a type of suffering servant, as he was sold into slavery by his brothers and then wrongfully jailed. Later on, God would elevate him to be the most powerful man in all of Egypt aside from Pharaoh himself! His road to the second most powerful man in the known world was filled with people who hated him for who he was, which was also prophesied about the coming Messiah.

Joseph was the firstborn, conceived from a mother who was barren until Yahweh intervened. He was raised in the Promised Land as his father's favorite son yet was hated by his own brothers due to his dreams about ruling over them one day. He was sent out by his father to his brothers where he brought back an evil report to his father. They rejected his dreams of ruling over them and tried to kill him. They ended up selling him for silver to Ishmaelite slave traders after they stripped off his robes (given to him by his father) and mocked him. He served as a slave until being tempted by Potiphar's wife and sent to jail. In jail, he was with two other prisoners and he refused to make a defense for himself but rather accepted God's plan for his life. He was then raised up to second in command of Egypt where he married a foreign wife and his dreams of ruling over his brothers came true.

How does Yeshua, the true Messiah ben Joseph compare? Well, He too was the firstborn of His father, conceived from a virgin mother by an intervention of Yahweh. He was raised in the Promised Land as His Father's favorite and only begotten son yet He was hated by his earthly brothers who did not receive Him or His "dreams" of ruling over them as their Savior. He was tempted by the devil and soon after His brothers then ordered to have him killed after Judas sold him for silver. His captors stripped His robes and mocked him as He was sent to the cross lowly and seemingly beaten. He was on the cross with two other prisoners and chose not to defend Himself but rather accept God's plan for His life. He was then raised up to eventually be the right hand of God where He will take us as his foreign bride and His visions of ruling over all of humanity will be fulfilled.

THIS CAN'+ BE ⊕UR GUY!

"This Messiah ben Joseph was prophesied to be hated and defeated! This couldn't be the same Messiah that all the other passages spoke about. There have to be TWO separate messiahs!" they thought and just like that the scholars and teachers of the day came to a comfortable conclusion. They all agreed that all of these messianic verses were talking about TWO separate messiahs instead of one. They were speaking about the Messiah ben Joseph and the Messiah ben David as separate people! Now I'm sure you can guess which of the two messiahs the people of Israel were expecting on Yeshua's entrance. That's right, Messiah ben David, the Conquering King. You can imagine their great disbelief upon seeing their Warrior-King being dragged through the streets bloody and beaten only to be hung on a cross and left for dead. To them, it was the worst thing that could have happened. Messiah ben Joseph fulfilled all of the prophecies about the Suffering Servant's arrival and life on earth. However, He did NOT fulfill all the prophecies about Messiah ben David.

The people of Israel made the mistake of focusing too closely on ONE side of a TWO-part dichotomy. Not only that, but their inability to understand the scriptures led to them missing one of the greatest mysteries of all. The Suffering Servant and the Conquering King are the SAME PERSON! They only had eyes for their Conquering King and despised the thought of their King suffering and being defeated unto death on the cross. You see, the Servant came to earth to provide a sacrifice for all of humanity's sins. His more humble, gentle and peaceful side came to pave the way for the future return where the Servant shall return as the KING.

Both sides of the dichotomy are needed. They are both parts of the same man (Yeshua the Christ). Without the servant, there is no king and without the king, there is no servant. Without the suffering, there is no conquering and without the conquering, there is no suffering. They are two sides of the same coin. Seeing as we are made in the image of Jesus our Lord, we too have the capacity for these same two sides within us. If you are not ready to serve then you are not ready to rule. The lowly will be exalted by our Father God and the proud will be brought down.

Yeshua coming as a servant was so scandalous to some of the religious people of the time that to THIS DAY there are people still waiting for their messiah's "first coming". They have missed out on one half of a whole and therefore have an incomplete view of their savior. Imagine if Jesus was not a servant. What if He only had the judgmental side of the king but lacked the compassionate side of the servant. That would not bode well for us sinners when we see Him face to face. Imagine if Yeshua was only Messiah ben Joseph and never Messiah ben David. What if Yeshua lacked the strength and holy power to rescue us from impending doom and only had loving forgiveness towards our enemies who sought to damn our souls. This would also not bode well for us. The same goes for every one of us. If we neglect the Conquering King side of ourselves then we lose the power and strength that comes with it. We are left too weak to face the fiery darts of the enemy or the perilous trials that await us in this life. We must also not forget to be the servant if we ever expect to rule as the king. We must submit to the TRUE king, Yahweh. Only through servitude will we learn what it really takes to be able to lead. If we do become leaders in any measure, we must never lose the part of us that is a servant. The second we favor one side over the other we run the risk of being a selfish leader or a weak powerless servant.

The main take away from this topic is to never forget that service is a part of leadership and your strength rests in being the royal son of the King. This must be remembered when times get tough. We are created in the image of our Father and He is the most selfless servant combined with the mightiest conqueror. Let us never forget this necessary dichotomy that is at the very core of the Knights of Yahweh's Army! Now that we have cut our teeth on our first dichotomy, let us delve even deeper and learn about the two animals that our King is likened to. One is an adorable, precious, and gentle creature while the other is a deadly, ferocious, and powerful creature. It is time we unveil the Lion and the Lamb!

CHAP+ER 3
THE LI⊕N AND THE LAMB

And one of the elders saith unto me, Weep not: behold,
the Lion of the tribe of Judah, the Root of David, hath
prevailed to open the book, and to loose the seven seals
thereof. And I beheld, and, lo, in the midst of the throne
and of the four beasts, and in the midst of the elders,
stood a Lamb as it had been slain, having seven horns
and seven eyes, which are the seven Spirits of God sent
forth into all the earth. – Revelation 5:5-6

ur Savior-King Jesus is referred to as a lion and also as a lamb many times throughout the holy writ. It is a beautiful and necessary dichotomy that has moved my heart for many years at the very thought. He is the perfect man, a Lion of the tribe of Judah and the sacrificial Lamb led to the slaughter for all mankind. You cannot separate the lion-like nature from the lamb-like nature and still have the same person. If you were to try to separate them you would have only a fragment or portion of the true person.

God's children and loyal subjects are created with the same traits in mind. It is with the lion's boldness that we take a stand for our faith or confront areas of sin in our lives. It is with the lamb's kind-hearted nature that we have the tenderness in dealing with a spouse or the gentleness to respond kindly in heated situations. Understanding each of the two roles is vital to have the correct picture of who we are called to be.

In mainstream Christianity you see what happens when one side is emphasized more than the other. Today's mainstream church depicts our king as the lamb only, thereby neutering Him of His lion-like nature. The mainstream version of Jesus is a milquetoast hippie who wouldn't hurt a fly and who is all about grace, grace and more grace. Does our King have grace? Of course! However, let us not forget that He also embodies *justice*. Does He exhibit peace? Indeed, He does. He also engages in *war* with the enemies to the throne.

The lamb seems to be the only side that mainstream Christianity is representing. They have this "safe" version of our Messiah that wouldn't even defend Himself or those He loves. They mistake meekness for weakness and it shows when you look at the men of the body. Today we have weak, style-conscious and effeminate sheep who act out Pharisee level displays of emotion to every pop-infused "worship" song being peddled in their so-called churches. Men who don't believe in self-defense, standing up for difficult issues like abortion, or standing firm against the acceptance of homosexuality. Most have prosperity focused and self-centered approaches to God Most High. It disgusts me. I ran out of my clothes fleeing from these places. Everything in this lamb doctrine feels forced and manufactured. I have even personally been to a "church" that was playing the Super Bowl right before evening service! Serving beer or have video game tournaments to attract the youth! Are you going to meet with your Father or to meet with wenches? Is church a holy ground to seek His face or a country club to meet your bros. I'll say this right now, IF YOUR CHURCH PLAYS THE SUPER BOWL OR SERVES ALCOHOL THEN IT IS NOT A CHURCH, IT IS A BAR!

And when he had made a scourge of small cords, he drove them all out of the temple, and the sheep, and the oxen; and poured out the changers' money, and overthrew the tables - John 2:15

Now that we got that out of the way we can talk about a less prevalent but just as important error: the over-emphasizing of the lion.

Though I speak with the tongues of men and of angels and have not charity **(love)**, I am become as sounding brass, or a tinkling cymbal. - 1 Corinthians 13:1 (commentary added)

Let your speech be always with grace, seasoned with salt, that ye may know how ye ought to answer every man - Colossians 4:6

If you speak the gospel or attack sin but you do it *without* the love of the lamb then you are doing damage. Without the meek and humble approach in our interactions with others, we become a vicious lion who recklessly slashes at everyone around him. We come from a position of having God's truth but the second that we add *pride* to that truth we become not only useless but harmful to the kingdom. Let us also not forget that no one wants to learn from someone with a "holier than thou" attitude that fails to display true love.

He that hath no rule over his own spirit is like a city that is broken down, and without walls. - Proverbs 25:28

If you cannot control your own spirit and emotions, you lack the components of the lamb. A city without walls is vulnerable to attack from all sides. How can you protect your own if you cannot even protect yourself? How can you teach others what you have yet to learn? I have struggled with this area for many years and I still strive to obtain more of the lamb in my life. We are in this together, my brothers and sisters and we have each other's backs. Let us now dissect the first part of this dichotomy, THE LION!

CHAPTER 4
THE LION OF THE TRIBE OF JUDAH

The lion pretended to be hurt and screamed in pain as his son bit at his paw. It was important to make the young one feel dangerous and confident so when the time came to hunt, he would be prepared. As they lay there, the hot sun fell and gave way to cool night and the son wandered off. The lion didn't go after him right way as to allow him to explore a bit. After a couple of minutes passed the lion stood to go retrieve his curious son when all of a sudden, he heard a loud and frantic yelp followed by several vicious growls.

As he sprinted and turned the corner, he saw his son in the mouth of the alpha hyena. He was blind to the eight other hyenas with him. Fear would not grip him this day. Only the need to save the one he loved. He ran forward full speed and tackled the alpha, pinning him to the ground and biting his throat as he saw his son careening through the air out of the filthy dog's mouth.

He ran and stood over his son. When the other hyenas encircled him, he then saw what they hovered over. It was the carcass of his bride, torn open and half consumed. He pushed his son behind him and let out a ferocious and terrifying roar. Two of the hyenas fled. He was still outnumbered, seven hyenas to one lion. He knew that there was a disadvantage...for them. He charged forward smashing and thrashing his way through the dogs as they tore at his flesh.

Before long the dust was settled and all that was left was a silhouette of the king of beasts walking away with his son's small shadow proudly walking beside him.

Revelation 5:5 refers to Jesus as the Lion of the tribe of Judah. Throughout our sacred texts, our King is referred to as a lion or being lion-like. We think of ferocity and royalty when thinking of a lion but that is not all that his magnificent beast represents. There are many other traits of a lion that show themselves also in our King. Let us now lay out the main traits of the lion mindset that are found throughout the Bible that are in line with our High Lord Jesus.

THE LION MINDSET

⊕ **Strong** - The lion's strength is unmatched amongst his peers just as our God's strength is unmatched.

A lion which is strongest among beasts, and turneth not away for any - Proverbs 30:30

⊕ **Regal, Royal and Having Authority** - The lion has dominion over all other beasts and authority over the land he rules, as does Jesus.

The lion hath roared, who will not fear? The Lord God hath spoken, who can but prophesy? - Amos 3:8

⊕ **Ferocious and Terrifying** - His roar strikes fear into the hearts of those who hear. Our God is also terrifying and ferocious to those who oppose Him.

> They shall walk after the Lord: he shall roar like a lion: when he shall roar, then the children shall tremble from the west. - Hosea 11:10

⊕ **Powerful** - There is no denying the power of the lion, whether bringing down an elephant or defending his cubs from packs of hyenas, his ferocity is widely known. It goes without saying that the God who created lions has more power than all lions combined.

> I reckoned till morning, that, as a lion, so will he break all my bones: from day even to night wilt thou make an end of me. - Isaiah 38:13

> For it increaseth. Thou huntest me as a fierce lion: and again, thou shewest thyself marvelous upon me. Job 10:16

⊕ **Bold and Fearless** - The lion is the paragon of bravery and has nothing to turn from in fear. Yahweh is also the Alpha and Omega among all creation. Nothing can cause Him to fear since nothing even comes close to Him is bravery or power.

> The wicked flee when no man pursueth: but the righteous are bold as a lion. - Proverbs 28:1

It seems only fitting that God would choose such an important, iconic, and strong beast to display several of His traits to His loyal vassals and sworn enemies alike. Our Father God, the Lion of the tribe of Judah, is an all-powerful and ferocious king. He inspires fear into the enemies of The Throne but also into His very own subjects. The fear that His enemies feel is the fear an animal feels while being stalked (Hosea 13:7, Lamentations 3:10). The dread of knowing something massive lies in wait as the anticipation of the kill strike makes their blood run cold. Finally, at just the right time He pounces from His hiding place and breaks the bones of his prey (Isaiah 38:13) then tears its flesh to shreds (Hosea 5:14). At the same time, to stand before the King or in His presence fills his own people with fear as well. However, it is a very different kind of fear. It is an awestruck reverence. It would be hard to lift up from a knee while He passes by, hoping to only touch the hem of His garment as the muscles in your neck refuse to allow your head to raise and observe such raw power lest you fall dead on the spot.

I have heard "I can't wait until I get to heaven because I have a bone to pick with God about such and such" or "When I get there I'm gonna ask him why this and this happened" from time to time by people who do not truly know Him. Arrogant and simple-minded. To think that you, a lowly man, could sit in the presence of your Creator and look Him in the eyes let alone demand anything is the most asinine thing I have ever heard! You would be completely undone just being in His presence. Without a word, your true sinful nature and secret sins lie bare before the one who you committed them against. Your only hope would be to bend the knee and beg for mercy. Much like a rabbit in front of the lion...the Lion of the tribe of Judah!

With the lion's mindset, we are able to have an unwavering approach to adversity. We are able to fight without quitting. We are able to stand against overwhelming odds. We are able to fall down seven times yet rise up eight. The lion does not show his power unless it is needed. He has the confidence of knowing his identity in Christ and knowing what truths his King says about him. He is royal and regal. The son of The True King. He does not debase himself with the simple pleasures of lesser animals. He does not eat the rotten carcasses of lust or return to the vomit that is a past sin. He has dominion over his spirit and control over his emotions. He makes the flesh subject to him just as he is subject to Yahweh.

CHAP✝ER 5
THE BRAVERY ⊕F HER⊕S

"I can hear them inside the bakery. If we go in there, they will slit our throats!" sobbed the young baker's daughter. "We have no other choice. For all we know your father is still in there." stressed the boy, who was just as terrified as she was. The girl was out with Rodrick, the blacksmith's son, swimming in Calten's Pond when they saw the smoke rising from over the hill.

At first, they thought the Inn was starting the night's dinner early. "That's odd" pondered the blacksmith's boy, "That looks like an awful lot of smoke...something is not right, we should lay eyes on the inn to make sure nothing is amiss." They soon after found out what caused the fire as they heard shouting from inside the bakery and the familiar voice of the girl's father growling from within. Before long the boy pushed open the door to reveal a terrible sight that would never be able to be cleansed from their young minds.

The two shifty looking travelers that were harassing the barmaid from the night before were standing over the girl's father with a sword drawn and dripping with blood while bread rolls and silver coins lay scattered all around the old baker. "RUN" shouted the father as the bigger of the two men started to chase them. The smaller, uglier one had her father by the scruff of his neck and started beating him, as the door swung shut and they made their escape. "GET THEM!" shouted the small one as they ran and hid behind the stables. They could hear the large man's footsteps stomping around searching for the two young friends. The boy's blood ran ice cold as he got a peek at the man from between wooden boards of the stables. The man was huge and corded with muscle. A dark green hood covered his face except for a scraggly red beard and a scar dancing down his thick neck.

The boy had never been more scared in his life and the girl started to squeeze his arm whispering "This is it; he will find us and I'll never see my mother again!" Just then the blacksmith's boy saw a rusted old short sword tucked in the back of one of the saddles. "No," he thought. "What am I going to do with that, I must be crazy? I'm not a knight!" Yet the girl's crying kept driving him forward like an unseen force pushing him toward the sword.

Finally, he grabbed the hilt as they heard the gigantic man laugh. "You two lovebirds think I won't find ya? HAHAHA...cough...cough...I'd never miss a chance to snag such a sweet prize as that young daisy ya have with ya, boy" The boy didn't know what happened but he felt a righteous fury well up in his chest as if seared by a hot brand. He felt as if the man would spot him since surely his eyes were ablaze from the fire inside of him. The girl held onto his leg as he pressed up against the stable's door from the inside. He still didn't know exactly what he had planned to do and was shocked that he had even grabbed the sword in the first place. But something inside of him knew...he had to do this. It had become his duty to stop this evil and protect his innocent young friend. Fear *gripped his heart and he started to shake as the giant was almost at the door. Although shaking, he NEVER took a step backward. Not ONE. He held his ground when finally, he saw the giant's fat hairy fingers pulling open the door.*

All he saw was the man's belt and the shine off of his bastard sword. It was like he was in a tunnel and nothing else mattered. The cries of the girl were still in his head but all he saw was the midsection of that giant, the shine of his sword and the fire in his own eyes. "FOUND YOU!!!" the man said as he reached a hand out to grab the boy who looked frozen in place but surprisingly angry for such a small kid. The hands closed around the boy's tunic as an image of the girl being taken by this man flashed before his eyes. "Father God help me any way you can!" prayed the boy in the quickest yet most meaningful prayer he had ever prayed.

THRUST! "AHHHHHRGGG!" The boy jammed the sword straight ahead as hard as he could and stepped forward into it as the sword slid just above the large man's belt and into his midsection. There was a small resistance then it slid right through as he heard a terrifying scream and felt the fat hairy fingers loosen their grip. "RUN LYLA!" he shouted at the girl and she wasted no time following the command.

The giant was slumped over as the boy withdrew the sword and stepped out of range of the big man. He was still shaking...still afraid. But fear did not rule that day. Duty ruled...COURAGE ruled. BRAVERY ruled and the boy drove the sword once more into the back of the giant and ran off after the girl...

Fear thou not; for I am with thee: be not dismayed; for I am thy God: I will strengthen thee; yea, I will help thee; yea, I will uphold thee with the right hand of my righteousness.
- Isaiah 41:10

The lion is brave and it is with this part of your spirit that you can face fear. You are *commanded* not to be afraid (Joshua 1:9). Cowardice is a sin (Revelation 21:8) and is unacceptable for the Knights in Yahweh's Army. Will you make mistakes and sometimes let fear prevail? Yes. Does this mean it is acceptable for fear to stay with you and impact your decisions? NO! The only fear that is present in the army of God is the fear of The Lord. The awestruck reverence that is appropriate when dealing with the Lord of Creation.

Now how does one be brave? You cannot be as brave as a lion if there is nothing to be brave about. Simple, right? So, don't pray for all your hardships and fears to be removed, rather pray to have the Lion's bravery to face them head-on! It is not your own bravery but the bravery bestowed upon you from your loving Father. Never take it for granted and never be so unwise as to think the bravery comes from any merit of your own.

Where can you exhibit this bravery? Speaking to someone about your faith is a good start. Standing up for righteousness in the workplace is another. Find ways to rout fear out of your life and replace it with bravery. Know that you are the son of the King and that King promises to protect you and see you through till the end.

Fear, doubt, and cowardice are weeds in the garden of life that spring up every now and then, they have to be diligently removed lest they overtake the garden and ruin its abundance. These things will pop up again and again and it is your duty to rebuke these thoughts and reject them through the wisdom in our Holy Scriptures.

The spiritual battle we are in often makes us tired and we grow weary of always fighting. Let me ask you, what is the alternative? Not fighting? Being overcome by the enemy? You have no excuses. The only option is to STAND AND FIGHT! Laziness on the battlefield gets you killed and worse gets the brothers around you killed as well. Will you let your laziness or weariness be the secret passage that the enemy sneaks in through? Will you let the weariness of doing good cause your brother to fall to the sword? You have no choice but to be in this fight. It is an unfortunate aspect of this fallen world we find ourselves in but take comfort knowing that you are a pilgrim in this world just passing through (1 Peter 2:11).

For our conversation (**citizenship**) is in heaven; from whence also we look for the Saviour, the Lord Jesus Christ - Philippians 3:20 (commentary added)

And let us not be weary in well doing: for in due season we shall reap, if we faint not. - Galatians 6:9

Hold on to the promise that if you continue on doing good **and** trusting The Lord then you shall reap reward in due season. Oh **yes**, there is a reward for this fight. Namely, a victorious entrance **into** eternity where you shall be assessed and addressed by your **King**. Picture it now. You report back to Him having finished well and **never** quit. You fought until the end and approach your Savior, ben**ding** the knee and becoming undone. He touches your shoulder and **you** hear that sacred line. "Well done good and faithful servant. You **have** been faithful until the end. Enter into the fruits of your enduranc**e**.... welcome...to the joy of The Lord." You rise only because He allows it **and** as tears stream down your face you wonder how you ever thought **even** for one second that it was hard because now you see clearer than **ever**... it was all worth it.

His lord said unto him, Well done, thou good and
faithful servant: thou hast been faithful over a few
things, I will make thee ruler over many things: enter
thou into the joy of thy lord. - Matthew 25:21

CHAPTER 6
THE
COUNTERFEIT LION

The Dark Lion's roar was filled with pride
But deep down he was fearful inside
He ambushed the weak as his dark heart grew colder
Always taking time to look over his shoulder
He knew that one day for his crimes he would pay
For the True Lion was never far away
As the Dark Lion's reign of terror grew stronger
The True Lion's bite could be held back no longer
As the Dark Lion roared and sought to devour
The True Lion chose to display his true power
The Dark One was shocked at the speed of the True
"I knew that one day I would come to see you"
The True Lion was silent as he tackled his foe
The Dark Lion yelped; the True Lion's eyes glowed
His jaws clamped shut on the Dark Lion that day
The True Lion knew that someday he would pay
The Dark Lion bled and was heard from no more
Neither was his bite and neither was his roar
Now think on this tale if you ever lose heart
The True Lion always tears the Dark One apart!

The dark lion, Satan, always seeks to steal the True King's ideas and use them for his own twisted desires. He is not original and uses the same old scams year after year. The sad part is we all still fall for these tired old tricks time and time again. Why fix it if it isn't broken, right? Well, it is time to wise up to the enemy's schemes and identify the mindset they use. Since the enemy does not have the capacity to create like our Father, the concept of the lion is stolen by the evil one as well. I will refer to that mindset as the "Counterfeit Lion" or "False Lion" from here on out.

The enemy's version of the lion has the following traits:

THE COUNTERFEIT LION MINDSET

⊕ **Overbearing** - The Counterfeit Lion is overbearing and hard to subdue. Jesus is a gentleman who always gives His people the right to choose their path.

> No man can enter into a strong man's house, and spoil his goods, except he will first bind the strong man; and then he will spoil his house. - Mark 3:27

⊕ **Powerful** - He was able to stand against the Archangel Michael. This shows that just like a lion, our enemy is extremely powerful and dangerous.

> Yet Michael the archangel, when contending with the devil he disputed about the body of Moses, durst not bring against him a railing accusation, but said, The Lord rebuke thee. - Jude 1:9

⊕ **Prideful** - He fell from heaven due to his pride and seeks to bring down anyone he can.

How art thou fallen from heaven, O Lucifer, son of the morning! How art thou cut down to the ground, which didst weaken the nations! For thou hast said in thine heart, I will ascend into heaven, I will exalt my throne above the stars of God: I will sit also upon the mount of the congregation, in the sides of the north: I will ascend above the heights of the clouds; I will be like the most High. Yet thou shalt be brought down to hell, to the sides of the pit. - Isaiah 14:12-15

⊕ **Deceitful** - The Counterfeit Lion's mindset was used to deceive Eve in the garden, promising a half-truth.

But I fear, lest by any means, as the serpent beguiled Eve through his subtlety, so your minds should be corrupted from the simplicity that is in Christ. - 2 Corinthians 11:3

⊕ **Cruel** - The Counterfeit Lion is always seeking people to destroy and devour.

Be sober, be vigilant; because your adversary the devil, as a roaring lion, walketh about, seeking whom he may devour: - 1 Peter 5:8

⊕ **Violent** - He will do anything to bring destruction to God's people.

The thief cometh not, but for to steal, and to kill, and to destroy: I am come that they might have life, and that they might have it more abundantly. - John 10:10

⊕ **Loveless** - He blinds the minds of those who have not yet found God. He ultimately desires to destroy the relationship between us and our Creator, possibly out of spite, revenge, or even to prove a point to our Father.

> In whom the god of this world hath blinded the minds of them which believe not, lest the light of the glorious gospel of Christ, who is the image of God, should shine unto them. - 2 Corinthians 4:4

⊕ **Weaker than the True Lion** - The Counterfeit Lion is no match for the authority given to us by God the Father. We may not be stronger than the dark one but our Father definitely is and He gives us the authority to subdue the enemy through His powerful name. Again, it is not your doing, but instead our Father's doing that deals with the enemy. Do not make the error of thinking you are the powerful one.

> Submit yourselves therefore to God. Resist the devil, and he will flee from you. - James 4:7

Purity. goodness.

The Dark Lion corners his unsuspecting victim. Although a full-grown ram would provide more than enough meat for him and his family, he decides against it. He goes for the unfair fight and corners the small lamb that got separated from the herd. He shreds its flesh to ribbons and smiles as the blood covers his muzzle. He attacks weary travels just for the sport of it. He plays nice until his prey is close enough then his toothy smile turns into a vicious roar as he betrays his would-be ally. He steals, kills, and destroys with no regard for the preciousness of life. Like a spurned lover tearing up the picture of a past love, he destroys the very picture or image of the Creator who banished him from His Kingdom for his traitorous acts.

Let me paint you a picture of a False Lion. If your manhood means being overly macho and dominating the weak, you are a False Lion. If you are all about yourself at the expense of others you are a False Lion. If you are cruel to others or violent then you are a False Lion. So, what now? Fix it! If you still have breath in your lungs then it is not too late. Repent on your knees to the Father. There is no time for self-pity. If you have several of these traits right now then have hope in the power of our King to change your heart. Don't sit and wallow in your shame. Take your brokenness to Him sooner rather than later. If you don't want to tackle these areas in our life then what are you doing reading this? When is the time to fix these things? Tomorrow?

> Boast not thyself of tomorrow; for thou knowest not
> what a day may bring forth. -Proverbs 27:1

You are not promised tomorrow and God may reclaim your soul this very day. Let's say your pride ruins a relationship with a loved one and you lose them. What more do you have to lose before you approach the throne and work on yourself with the King of Kings Himself? Will you wait till after your violence kills someone to then address it? Don't be a fool. Address these things now while there is still time.

Don't sit and wallow
• self-pity

CHAP+ER 7
S⊕BER AND VIGILAN+

Ser Highbear stared into the bottom of his tankard and saw the drink sloshing to and fro as he felt sorely vexed for himself. He had been removed from the King's Guard by account of his habit of arriving for duty still smelling like sour wine from the night before. His father was a drunkard before him and he ofttimes thought that he had inherited the foul habit. Just then, a fair maiden entered into the tavern and set her eyes wantonly upon Ser Highbear for no apparent reason. He was not one to question the affections of a maiden, let alone one so fair.

"My good Ser! Art thou not one of the King's Guard? Have I not seen thee in His Lordship's castle, protecting the Royal Family? Why dost thou tarry here in this lowly place?" asked the Maiden. "I have been removed on account of my drunkenness, so I have resolved myself to drown my sorrows in the drink furthermore. Wouldst

thou join in my sad celebration?" mumbled the disgraced knight. "Good Ser, I have only arrived this night to retrieve wine for my master. Mayhaps thou shalt return with me...surely there shall be room enough in MY bedchambers..." flirted the maid.

Lord Highbear should have known something was amiss from how forward the maiden was being. The dagger by her hip should have been the second clue but the drink had dulled his senses and empowered his lusts. "I shall follow you, oh fair one. After all, what kind of knight leaves a maiden to walk alone in the darkness?" burped the knight, wiping wine from his chin. "Right this way Ser Knight," she said as she took his hand upon hers and led him out into the cold dark night. It was not long before two bandits surrounded the knight and the maiden unawares to make off with the knight's coin.

Before Ser Highbear could draw his blade, the bandits fell upon him knocking him asunder. They pinned him to the ground and as he looked up all he could see was a cruel smile on the "maiden's" lips as she drew forth her blade and ran him through.

The commander of the enemy's armies, Satan, tries to mimic the Lion in many ways. He walks about *as* a roaring lion seeking whom he may devour (1 Peter 5:8). The Counterfeit Lion is mangy, feral and fights for the scraps of the true Alpha, Yeshua.

> Be sober, be vigilant; because your adversary the devil,
> as a roaring lion, walketh about, seeking whom he may
> devour - 1 Peter 5:8

The command in this verse when dealing with this false lion is to be sober and vigilant. Being sober means to be serious, studious, level-headed, and to be of a *clear mind*. Anything that affects our judgment and decision-making skills should be avoided at all costs. If we are to avoid and unclear mind, we must know what exactly gives us an unclear mind.

THE UNCLEAR MIND

Fear, Lust

⊕ **Alcohol and Drugs (sometimes even pharmaceuticals)**
- These substances can dull the senses and inhibitions making us vulnerable to attack.

> And be not drunk with wine, wherein is excess; but be
> filled with the Spirit; - Ephesians 5:18

⊕ **Sin** - Sin leaves us blinded by our own lusts and surrounded by lies, unable to see the truth. As we push deeper toward our sin, we have fewer and fewer qualms about what we are sacrificing along the way.

> If we say that we have fellowship with him, and walk in
> darkness, we lie, and do not the truth: - 1 John 1:6

⊕ **Lust** - Lust keeps us bound to serving our flesh and weakens our spirit. Your judgment and decision making are driven by your lust instead of your reason and knowledge of the Word of God.

> For all that is in the world, the lust of the flesh, and the
> lust of the eyes, and the pride of life, is not of the Father,
> but is of the world. - 1 John 2:16

⊕ **Anger** - Anger also blinds us to the truth and keeps us serving the flesh instead of spirit. In a blind rage, a man will do many things he would never do if he were not angry. This is a short road to committing murder.

> Be ye angry, and sin not: let not the sun go down upon your
> wrath: Neither give place to the devil. - Ephesians 4:26-27

⊕ **Greed** - Greed keeps us in a never-ending cycle of chasing material possessions and never being able to be content in any form. We tighten the spiritual noose a little further with each step we take towards our earthly gain.

> And he said unto them, Take heed, and beware of covetousness: for a man's life consisteth not in the abundance of the things which he possesseth. - Luke 12:15

⊕ **Pride** - Pride causes us to serve ourselves and stops any chance at spiritual growth we may have. It makes you a slave to your own ego and elevates you above the Word of God. It is only a matter of time before a prideful man makes decisions solely based on himself with no regard for God.

> A man's pride shall bring him low: but honour shall uphold the humble in spirit. - Proverbs 29:23

Many of these things, in addition to numerous others, are to be completely abstained from if you want to have a clear head on the field of battle. Like a knight with sand in his eyes, an unclear mind will have you swinging in the wind when you should be striking true.

Let's touch on vigilance. Being vigilant means keeping a careful watch for possible danger or difficulties. The value of this in your life goes without saying. Just like riding a horse. You cannot take your eyes off the road. In battle, you cannot look away from your opponent. It calls for you to be proactive and be constantly on the lookout for danger. Not just waiting for it to fall upon you unawares. How much easier will it be to slay a dragon when it is younger and smaller as opposed to letting it grow out of control and then trying to face it? The same goes for our sin. One of the main things that any sin stem from is pride. It is on that note that we move on to our next section.

CHAP✝ER 8
LI⊕N'S PRIDE

"How you are fallen from heaven,
O Lucifer, son of the morning!
How you are cut down to the ground,
You who weakened the nations!
For you have said in your heart:
'I will ascend into heaven,
I will exalt my throne above the stars of God;
I will also sit on the mount of the congregation
On the farthest sides of the north;
I will ascend above the heights of the clouds,
I will be like the Most High.'
Yet you shall be brought down to Sheol,
To the lowest depths of the Pit.
Isaiah 14:12-15

ne of the deadliest traits of the False Lion is *pride*. It is the absolute antithesis of humility. Pride will tell you that *you* know best. It causes you to speak on a matter before you even hear it. It causes you to be offended at the drop of a hat. It closes ears and hardens hearts. It blinds you to correction and puts you as the god of your life instead of the God of the Bible. Pride is a bandit that gives a weary traveler wrong direction and steers him into a trap. It is an open pit with never-ending spikes to keep you ensnared to your own way over anyone else's.

Pride will puff you up and make you have a higher opinion of yourself than you should. It is false confidence and causes you to boast about your abilities, possessions, appearance, accolades, or a myriad of other worthless earthly things. The only thing we should boast about is our Savior the Lord Jesus Christ. Pride seeks to take the glory that belongs to Father for ourselves.

> But he that glorieth, let him glory in the Lord. - 2 Corinthians 10:17

Pride only looks out for itself and turns you into the most selfish person in the room. It takes away your ability to truly care about others or even listen to what they have to say. You become one of those people in a conversation who is just waiting to talk and most likely about yourself. You loudly proclaim your grand opinions as if they are the only one that has any value. It makes you think that you are the only person that is right and everyone else has it wrong. It makes you become your own god. This is full-blown idolatry!

Pride has its beginnings all the way back in the third chapter of Genesis. The serpent sought to undermine God's authority and commands and replace them with his own lies and deception. He was immediately cursed and then issued a prophecy of Yeshua's arrival on earth to rectify what he had done. The enemy puts his wants and desires over the desires of the Creator. By doing so he forever changed humanity. Adam and Eve played their part by going assuming they knew best when choosing to side with the Serpent instead of trusting the God of the Bible. This sin is completely pervasive in the fallen world and continues into modernity.

I would go so far as to say nearly all sins can be traced back to pride and idolatry. Any time you decide to go against God's will and do your own, that is pride and idolatry. You are exalting your will over the Father's. That is the deadliest road you can travel aside from flat out war on God. Look at the pride in the Tower of Babel incident. Nimrod sought to storm the gates of heaven and make war on God. His pride went unchecked and festered like a flesh-eating disease for so long that he thought he could take on Yahweh. Our adversary the devil was created perfect and that still did not make him exempt from this sin. The beauty and splendor that The Lord created in him caused him to be corrupted by his love for himself. Yet, it was by no merit of his own that he was created perfect and beautiful. It was the Father who made him that way in the first place, yet he still gave in to pride and boasted about it.

> Thou wast perfect in thy ways from the day that thou wast created, till iniquity was found in thee. - Ezekiel 28:15

> Thine heart was lifted up because of thy beauty, thou hast corrupted thy wisdom by reason of thy brightness: I will cast thee to the ground, I will lay thee before kings, that they may behold thee. - Ezekiel 28:17

Did you know God opposes the proud? Did you know he detests those with a proud heart and promises that they will not go unpunished? Is your pride so precious that you choose to war against Father God Himself!? What other way is there to look at it? If you struggle with pride just realize that you have to humble yourself and let go of your own selfish way or risk King Yahweh humbling you. You don't want to step out from under your Father's hedge of protection. If you walk your own way and become so preoccupied with yourself, you risk stepping out of the parameters that your King has set for you. You are walking into enemy territory.

> Every one that is proud in heart is an abomination to the Lord: though hand join in hand, he shall not be unpunished. - Proverbs 16:5

But he giveth more grace. Wherefore he saith, God resisteth the proud, but giveth grace unto the humble. - James 4:6

A true believer should value others over themselves. This is a constant choice that has to be made. Just like your salvation, it is not a choice that you make once and never think about it again. You have to continuously decide to walk in Father's ways. One of those ways is putting others above yourself.

Let nothing be done through strife or vainglory, but in lowliness of mind let each esteem others better than themselves. - Philippians 2:3

It is Yeshua's will that we esteem others above ourselves and He showed it by His actions all throughout the Bible. When asked what was the greatest commandment of all He gave two. Love God with everything you have and love your neighbor as yourself. In other words, treat your neighbor just as good as you would treat yourself. Now if you don't have a good view of yourself how can you then treat others any better? I would go and read every passage about what Father God says about His children. With an understanding of the truth and of your true value, you can then be able to treat others better.

Then one of them, which was a lawyer, asked him a question, tempting him, and saying, Master, which is the great commandment in the law? Jesus said unto him, Thou shalt love the Lord thy God with all thy heart, and with all thy soul, and with all thy mind. This is the first and great commandment. And the second is like unto it, Thou shalt love thy neighbor as thyself. On these two commandments hang all the law and the prophets. - Matthew 22:35-40

Do you really think yourself so wise that you know better than the King of Kings? Think of all the times where you chose wrong. Don't relive them just think. That is what it's like when you lead. In the state we are born into, we gravitate towards sin. Only a morally perfect creator can make moral laws and say what is right and what is wrong. Nothing you do can add a day to your life or even a hair to your head. Sometimes we can be our own worst enemies as our flesh rages on and we continue to feed it making it stronger than our spirit.

Let's talk practicality. How would you start applying this right now? Well, if you have a spouse or a significant other you have your work cut out for you. Any time there is a disagreement you need to pause before you react. You need to ask yourself "is this worth winning." Think about how you can make your loved one's life better and stop acting like *they* are just there to make *your* life better. When your boss is coming down on you in the workplace there is definitely a time to stand up for yourself and especially when it comes to your faith. However, if your boss is just giving you attitude, your pride will start to rear its ugly head and say "I don't deserve this!", "They can't treat me like that!" or "You're one to talk!" Your flesh unchecked will naturally gravitate towards sin. You don't need to feed your flesh and give your boss a piece of your mind. Start denying those impulses and pray for the Father to give you a couple of seconds to pause before you go right to reacting.

Fasting is a great way to starve the flesh not only physically but spiritually. You can put it back into subjection to your spirit. Fasting and consuming the Word of God really puts the power of the flesh into perspective. At first, my flesh would be screaming at me after only four hours of not eating. "Feed me, I'm starving!" After eight hours my flesh tells me that I am practically dying. But man does not live off bread alone but by the words of God (Matthew 4:4). Sometime after the first day of fasting my body then gives up. It is under the command of my spirit. It stops sending pleas of hunger to the brain and quietly moves along with its day. For me personally, it is hard to remain prideful when I am fasting. It quiets me down and forces me to hear the spiritual more than the carnal. It slows me down and realigns my priorities.

In conclusion, pride much like any sin, it is a fire in a dry land. Once it is burning it is easier to handle sooner rather than later. If your sin fire is out of control, it is not too late to turn to Yeshua and ask Him to help put it out. It's never too late to repent. Snuff out your sin while it is starting to kindle and don't wait for it to turn into a raging inferno and burn you and everyone else along the way to repentance.

Humble yourselves in the sight of the Lord, and he shall lift you up. - James 4:10

CHAP✝ER 9
THE LAⅯB WH⊕
WAS SLAIN

The king had yet to choose an heir to his throne as he had not been blessed with any natural sons. Today was the day the realm had been waiting for...the day he would choose a successor. A righteous man to rule the kingdom after he had gone to be with The Lord. Two of the king's finest warriors returned from battle to report their deeds to their king. The first knight was the undefeated Lionheart of Cattersberg. He was the older of the two and the more decorated warlord. Lionheart had never been unhorsed, bested in tournament, or bested on the battlefield. He walked up to the king, back straight as an arrow in his shining mahogany-red plated armor with golden trim. On his breastplate stood the lion's head crest of his house in such detailed work that it put all of the land's artists to great shame.

Lionheart saluted the king and began his report. "My Lord, we have taken the Southlands. We attacked the legion of barbarians as they held their dark mass. We took them unawares and made short work of them as we put the whole city to the sword in your name. We then marched east to Scarswood and reclaimed the farmlands from the pagans that dwelt there. We decimated their forces and dashed all of their altars to pieces. The only regret I have is that we had no time to send the wounded home to their families as we needed to press on. We lost many of our weaker men but in exchange, we conquered the surrounding kingdoms and secured the lands for your future king, whomever you choose."

The king saluted the brave knight and addressed him. "Lionheart you have fought valiantly and bravely. Without your conquests, our kingdom would be surrounded on every side by enemies to the throne. You have secured safety for our people and for this I thank you. However, there is one thing that brings me great sadness upon hearing. You have let your wounded brethren die due to you being so set on your goals of conquest. Their families will care little for the land you secured when they realize their loved ones will not be returning home from your great campaign. May you learn from this grand error and think of the greater vision when you are fulfilling your quest. Now, my lord Auric St. Lambros, rise from your bended knee and issue me your report."

Auric St. Lambros humbly knelt during the entirety of his dear friend Lionheart's report. He loved him like a brother and had missed his companionship since the war started. His tattered hand-stitched sigil of a lamb and a cross was coming undone from his dirty tunic. Auric St. Lambros was a renowned knight of the realm but far more people knew of his deeds than they did his name. He was often seen among the townspeople escorting the elderly home or settling disputes in the taverns. He was the first to arrive when someone would complain of bandits stealing their sheep and the last to leave during the weekly prayer services in the temple. The priests would be getting ready to head home as they would see Auric sweeping the floors of the temple with a smile on his face, lost in private prayer.

Auric stood to make his report. "Greetings Your Majesty. It is with a heavy heart that I bring my report this day for I fear it will not live up to the task you assigned me. You have told me to secure the safety of the towns in our immediate vicinity while Lord Lionheart traveled abroad and I must say, we are in a sad state of affairs. The people in the town are downtrodden over the recent burnings of the crops at the hands of our evil neighbors. They are extremely hungry and it was all I could do to give them food from my own estate's storehouses while I tracked down the culprits. I failed to capture both raiding parties due to their attacking from both the east and west. I was only able to capture the attackers from the eastern gate and they await your judgment in the castle dungeon."

"I am terribly grieved to ask something from a king who has blessed me beyond measure. I do not wish to seem ungrateful as I make my request known. I ask His Royal Lordship if he would be so kind as to keep my payment for the errand and instead open His Lordship's storehouses to the publicans once a week. I know I ask a lot however the townsfolk are falling apart at the seams and I would hate for the king's loyal subjects to live day to day hating the very existence God has granted them." As Lambros finished his speech he bowed his head back down, wiping his eyes and waiting for a reply.

The king addressed Auric St. Lambros with tears welling in his own eyes. "You were unable to apprehend both camps of raiders? All because you were feeding and protecting the peasants? My dear boy, the duty that I had assigned to you pales in comparison to the compassion you have shown this day. You have selflessly given grain from your own storehouses and now you offer to sacrifice your payment to further help those in need? I shall give you double the amount of food you ask for from the castle granary and you shall receive the gold I promised you for the task I sent you on." said the very taken aback king.

"This brings me to my next matter before we end our gathering. The time is nye to choose my heir" exclaimed the king as both knights nodded to each other, ready for their lives to be forever changed. "Lord Lionheart, you have served the throne well and conquered more lands than any of our ancestors before us. For this, you are to be well appreciated and well rewarded. To you, I give the first fruits of the land which you have conquered. And I give to you also the hand of my daughter Lady Patricia to be wed to you. You shall become a part of my family on paper as you already have been in heart."

"As for Auric St. Lambros, to give to you the hand of my dear daughter Lady Mary. For, ever since she has laid eyes on you, her thoughts have been on no other. Lastly, I have a just reward for your deeds in selflessly helping the townsfolk and not thinking it too far below your station to help those in need, as any true knight should. To you, I give you the crown and title of...HEIR TO THE THRONE!"

The people in the great hall all fell silent as they could barely fathom what happened. The less skilled and less famous of the two knights was crowned king? Everyone had always assumed it would be great Lord Lionheart that would rule over them. Out of the silence came the clapping of one man...Lord Lionheart.

The lion knight spoke with a booming voice, "Let me be the first to bend the knee to my brother in arms Auric St. Lambros. I have always known him to be the better man and to be honest I have looked up to him for the better part of our adulthood. He was always most generous when dealing with any of the commoners. He never thought a duty below his station for he never quite cared about what his station was. He is a true servant and I will gladly protect these lands with my armies as they are under the banner of his house, the lamb and the cross."

The crowd burst into cheers and the king stood and hugged them both squeezing ever so tightly as he had never felt quite as happy as that moment. The moment where the KING saw fit to CROWN the LAMB instead of the LION.

We have examined the lion side of lion/lamb dichotomy and it is now time to learn about the kinder and gentler side. It is with a soft heart that we now take a look at the mindset of The Lamb. Yeshua is referenced as the lamb thirty-one times in the Book of Revelation alone (KJV). Years and years of sacrificing animals (lambs included) that were without spot or blemish had led up to the one ultimate sacrifice...Jesus the Lord's Christ, hanging on that tree. Take a moment to really think about what we are about to get into. This was the single greatest event in all history causing every day before and after to be counted as either Before Christ (B.C.) or by the Latin phrase "anno domini" (A.D., in the year of The Lord). The thought that while we were yet sinners He still went forward and rescued us from the clutches of death should move us at the very thought. Some say that He came to take our place in the heavenly courtroom and receive our punishment. No, no, it is more precisely described as us being under the command of the second death (separation from God for eternity) and being *ransomed* and put us under His service (Matthew 20:28). Now we are appointed only the first death and are spared the second. And all of this while we still had yet to commit our first sin!

There has never been a greater sacrifice in all of time than the innocent Jesus giving His life for guilty sinners who He called His friends (John 15:13). The Father exalted the Son because the Son humbled Himself (1 Peter 5:6-7). There has never been a humbler act than the Royal

King coming down to Earth and showing His subjects how to be the ultimate servant. He took on flesh and walked among us. What other gods have done this? What other gods spared us the earning of our salvation through works? There is nothing more astonishing than seeing the Lion of the tribe of Judah become The Lamb that was slain. Wow...thank you Yeshua for your sacrifice...words are not enough to show how eternally grateful we are. Hopefully, we get to spend the rest of eternity showing you just how much it meant to us.

> Greater love hath no man than this, that a man lay down his life for his friends. - John 15:13

> Humble yourselves therefore under the mighty hand of God, that he may exalt you in due time - 1 Peter 5:6-7

Earthy fathers will fail us and hurt us and although they may try their best, they will fall short. Our Heavenly Father will never fall short. He will never hurt us and He will always love us. Whatever scars our earthly fathers have left in our lives, our Heavenly Father will heal with His never-ending love. If your earthly father walked out on you and your family please take great comfort in knowing that Father God has been there from the start and will never, ever, EVER think about leaving you, let alone actually do it.

King Jesus came on the scene as the sinless and spotless Lamb of God who would take away the sin of the world (John 1:29) and was led like a *sheep* to the slaughter (Isaiah 53:7) where He silently accepted His death sentence. Yeshua's first coming on this earth was as "Messiah ben Joseph," The Suffering Servant. Yahweh first extended the olive branch to humanity through His son Yeshua, The Suffering Servant. Now let us see what traits the Lamb side of the dichotomy represents:

THE LAMB MINDSET

⊕ **Meekness** - Jesus submitted to His Father and showed restraint and control of spirit when dealing with others.

The meek will he guide in judgment: and the meek will he teach his way. -Psalm 25:9

Take my yoke upon you, and learn of me; for I am meek and lowly in heart: and ye shall find rest unto your souls - Matthew 11:29

⊕ **Humility** - Jesus came as a sheep and sacrificed His life even though He had the power to create the heavens and the Earth (Philippians 2:6-11).

Humble yourselves in the sight of the Lord, and he shall lift you up. - James 4:10

⊕ **Obedience** - The best lamb is the one that is obedient to its shepherd's call. We should also be obedient to our heavenly Shepherd's call.

He is in the way of life that keepeth instruction: but he that refuseth reproof erreth. - Proverbs 10:17

Jesus answered and said unto him, if a man love me, he will keep my words: and my Father will love him, and we will come unto him, and make our abode with him. - John 14:23

Ye shall walk in all the ways which the Lord your God hath commanded you, that ye may live, and that it may be well with you, and that ye may prolong your days in the land which ye shall possess. - Deuteronomy 5:33

⊕ **People-person** - Jesus came to be among His people and to ransom them from the clutches of death.

Beloved, if God so loved us, we ought also to love one another. - 1 John 4:11

A new commandment I give unto you, that ye love one another; as I have loved you, that ye also love one another. - John 13:34

⊕ **Kind-hearted and Gentle** - Jesus was and is the perfect example on how to treat others. He was always kind-hearted, stood up for the weak, and treated others with gentleness even while they were sinners.

And be ye kind one to another, tenderhearted, forgiving one another, even as God for Christ's sake hath forgiven you. - Ephesians 4:32

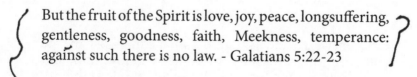

But the fruit of the Spirit is love, joy, peace, longsuffering, gentleness, goodness, faith, Meekness, temperance: against such there is no law. - Galatians 5:22-23

⊕ **Dependent on the Shepherd** - Jesus did nothing without His Father, The Shepherd.

> Then answered Jesus and said unto them, Verily, verily, I say unto you, The Son can do nothing of himself, but what he seeth the Father do: for what things so ever he doeth, these also doeth the Son likewise. - John 5:19

CHAP+ER IØ
THE MEEK SHALL INHERI+ THE EAR+H

Blessed are the meek: for they shall inherit the earth. -
Matthew 5:5

Meekness - the fact or condition of being meek; submissiveness
Synonyms: patience, long-suffering, forbearance, resignation

I saiah 53:7 says that He (Jesus) was oppressed, and he was afflicted, yet he opened not his mouth; like a lamb that is led to the slaughter, and like a sheep that before its shearers are silent, so he opened not his mouth. Yeshua could have completely decimated His captors and walked away without even so much as lifting a finger. But He didn't. He was silent. This is a great display of meekness. He had more than enough power to fight back but instead, He chose to submit to those seeking His destruction. For He knew that through submitting many would be saved.

Meekness should in no way be confused for weakness. Weakness is having a deficiency in an area making it less strong than other areas. Meekness is restraint. It is being slow to speak and making sure you have thought a matter through before choosing to speak on it.

> Seest thou a man that is hasty in his words? There is more hope of a fool than of him. - Proverbs 29:20

> He that answereth a matter before he heareth it, it is folly and shame unto him. - Proverbs 18:13

I cannot stress to you enough just how important it is to hold your tongue. On the field of battle, a knight's heroic war steed is one of his most powerful allies. His majestic mane flows freely as his stone hard hooves pound the ground causing the sound of thunder to rage into the ears of all who stand before him. Yet, as strong as this beast is, he is controlled by the small piece of metal in his mouth called the bit (James 3:3). As a child of God, created in His image, we are like Him in many ways. One of the ways we are like Him is the power that we are able to issue forth with our words. Death and life are in the power of the tongue and we can choose to bring forth life or death based on what words we choose and when we choose to say them.

> Death and life are in the power of the tongue: and they that love it shall eat the fruit thereof. - Proverbs 18:21

> Wherefore, my beloved brethren, let every man be swift to hear, slow to speak, slow to wrath - James 1:19

One misplaced word can cost you your job, relationship, or your peace among many other things. At the same time, one wisely placed word can absolve someone of a crime, clear your name, defend the weak, or even help you to take a stand for the Heavenly Kingdom. Do not take this lightly? Our God does not. Do not let cursing or foul joking come out of your mouth. You are a child of the King, not a court jester, so it is time to act like it!

Here are some ways of speaking you should steer clear of:

- ⊕ Lying
- ⊕ Cursing
- ⊕ Inappropriate Speech
- ⊕ Filthy Jokes
- ⊕ Gossip
- ⊕ Slander
- ⊕ Watering down or softening matters of the Kingdom
- ⊕ And most of all *anything* that you speak that is *without love* (1 Corinthians 15:1)

Neither filthiness, nor foolish talking, nor jesting, which are not convenient: but rather giving of thanks. - Ephesians 5:4

Finally, brethren, whatsoever things are true, whatsoever things are honest, whatsoever things are just, whatsoever things are pure, whatsoever things are lovely, whatsoever things are of good report; if there be any virtue, and if there be any praise, think on these things. Those things, which ye have both learned, and received, and heard, and seen in me, do: and the God of peace shall be with you. - Philippians 4: 8-9

Something else that stands in the way of us and a meek heart is pride. God hates a proud heart. Pride comes natural to humans however humility must be learned and practiced. It is through humility that we grow in our faith and in our maturity in The Lord. It is through the fire and flames that we are refined and are brought out stronger than ever. Let the Father's loving correction wash over you as you learn to weather the storm. Like a lighthouse in the middle of the ocean as the waves beat against its side, take the hits and stand strong. Like a stalwart defender holding his shield steady as slash after slash from the evil Gibborim rain down onto his shield sending sparks and paint chips everywhere. Hold your shield high. We know that God cannot be tempted nor does He tempt us (James 1:13). So that leaves only loving correction and the testing of our faith that remains. Do not resist His loving corrections. The Knights of Yahweh's Army will pass these tests and come out on the other side with scars and battered armor as we bend the knee in victory to our Heavenly King!

Who, being in the form of God, thought it not robbery to be equal with God: But made himself of no reputation, and took upon him the form of a servant, and was made in the likeness of men: And being found in fashion as a man, he humbled himself, and became obedient unto death, even the death of the cross. Wherefore God also hath highly exalted him, and given him a name which is above every name: That at the name of Jesus every knee should bow, of things in heaven, and things in earth, and things under the earth; And that every tongue should confess that Jesus Christ is Lord, to the glory of God the Father.
- Philippians 2:6-11

CHAPTER II
TRUST, FEAR, AND DEPENDENCE ON THE SHEPHERD

When my dearest friends all laughed at me for giving up the drink,
I never look back once or even cared what they would think.

When I left that wayward woman that I once loved so dear,
I knew that I was better off because my Lord was near.

When let go from my job in town I never became mad,
'Cuz then I had free Saturdays for Sabbaths with my Dad.

But the day that I lost my lover, my best friend, and my wife,
T'was the day I cursed the Heavens for the sparing of my life.

Why, oh, why did He keep me here with half my heart left in a grave?
I had thought that I could trust the one who was so mighty to save.

As I lay there on my knees with the tears soaking in my eyes,
I felt a peace enter the room with a parting of the skies.

The Lord arrived with a quiet voice freezing me in place.
He said, "Dear son, why do you have that look upon your face?"

I said "Dear Lord I had trusted you my whole life until now,"
"I sacrificed it all for you ever since I made that vow."

"And I know you say to trust you and your ways are my own."
"But I never thought you'd call her home and leave me here alone."

But then I felt a gentle hand brush up against my cheek.
A peace filled me and stopped my tears that lasted for a week.

He said, "Dear son, what is there that I have not given you?"
I gave you life, I gave you breath and I gave her to you too."

"You have trusted me for all these years through ridicule and shame."
"I have kept you safe and prospered you and even cleared your name."

"Now all your trust and all your pain has led up to this day,"
"Where what I have prepared you for, I will make clear today"

"Because you've always trusted me and bore my name so well,"
"I trusted you with the pain of loss so you'd have something to tell."

"Now go unto your countrymen and tell them all the tale,"
"Of how you trusted me for years and never did you fail."

"I give to you and take from you and in the end, you'll surely see,"
"That everything I did for you prepared you for eternity."

salm 18:2 very concisely sums up the three areas that we are about to expand upon. The verse says "The Lord is my rock, my fortress, and my deliverer." The Lord is our rock and rocks give a sure-footed place to stand. The rock represents His stability and trustworthiness. He is then described as our fortress. When we have trusted in Yahweh, we then start to make our home in Him and depend on Him as we would depend on the protection of a formidable castle tower. Lastly, the verse describes our Father as a deliverer. When we trust that Yahweh will deliver us and also depend on Him to do so, we are showing the fear of The Lord. We are showing that fear by acknowledging that there is no one else that we put our faith in to deliver us. *He* is our deliverer and no one else will do.

> The Lord is my rock, and my fortress, and my deliverer;
> my God, my strength, in whom I will trust; my buckler,
> and the horn of my salvation, and my high tower. -
> Psalm 18:2

The second part of the verse goes into other details that are relevant to this chapter. We should take note when it says "...my God, my strength, in whom I will trust; my buckler, and the horn of my salvation, and my high tower." First, we note that He is our strength. It is not of our own strength that we are able to have victory in this life but through His strength. He gives strength to the weary and increases the power of the weak (Isaiah 41:10). Next, we see the use of the word buckler. A buckler is a type of shield. Your more common shield is broader and protects the body but the buckler is a smaller shield worn on the arm that was used mainly to block or parry an opponent's strikes. A buckler was also held out in front of you and could be used as an *offensive* weapon to punch an enemy with. In Psalm 91:4 God says "His truth shall be your shield and buckler." So not only will His truth shield our spiritual body from attack but will also be used to parry the fiery darts of the enemy and punch the evil one right in his wicked teeth!

Next, we see that God is the "horn" of our salvation. Horns are representative of power, strength, and in some cases aggressiveness (think animal kingdom). Here we see horn being used in the context of a musical instrument. A war trumpet to announce to everyone that has ears to hear to "LET IT BE KNOWN, THIS CHILD IS A CHILD OF THE MOST HIGH YAHWEH!" If that doesn't give you security, I don't know what will! And lastly, Yahweh says He is our "high tower". This is an obvious one that shows we can take refuge in Him and trust that we are safe behind the formidable walls of His loving arms. And now we will dive into the three main topics of our discussion.

TRUS+

Prayer against Jezebel Spirit

The first topic we need to address is trust. Trust can be a sensitive topic for some people as it usually brings up feelings of betrayal, abandonment, or broken trust. We all carry many scars from our brothers and sisters that we have accumulated over the years of our perilous pilgrimage throughout this world. Some of us lost trust early in life when a parent abandoned us and walked out on the family. Some had parents who lied to them and could never be counted on to keep their word. Others have trust scars from later in life due to being cheated on by a lover. Few blades can cut as deep as the blade of betrayal. This fallen world only offers a shadow of heavenly things so we must look to the skies for the true form of these godly principles and trust is no different.

True biblical trust is usually focused on The Lord. He is the guideline for how we are to act out our lives and He is the only one we can ever truly trust without a doubt and without fail. We are told that it is better to trust in God than to trust in man (Psalm 118:8). We aren't even able to fully trust *ourselves* seeing as our heart is deceitfully wicked and no man can know it (Jeremiah 17:9). So, what are we left with? We are told not to lean on our own understanding but to trust The Lord with *all* of our heart (Proverbs 3:5-6).

Trust in the LORD with all thine heart, and lean not unto thine own understanding. - Proverbs 3:5-6

The moment you start the conscious and deliberate *choice* to trust The Lord, your life will change in many ways. This is not a one-time choice but rather a series of many choices that we will have to decide to make for the rest of our lives. This is crucial! You must *consistently* choose to trust Yahweh every single time a situation to do so presents itself. When you decide to trust what God says in His word, you can start to eliminate many snares that the enemy sets in your path. For example, The Lord *commands* us to be anxious about nothing (Philippians 4:6-7). If we understand anxiety as being something commanded against, we are able to stop feeling sorry for ourselves and treat it as such. By changing our perspective, we can formulate a new plan of attack.

Think of it this way, let's say you have a job interview which you are worried about and it is causing you to lose sleep. You are familiar with the scriptures that say to cast your burdens on The Lord so you pray a simple prayer. "Lord please take my anxiety about this situation away, I put this problem into your hands and I trust that you will work it out for good since I love you and follow you with my whole heart. Amen." Now if the second you cast your burden on Yahweh you turn around and pick it back up, you are not trusting in The Lord! Yes, these things can be hard and mistakes can happen but don't cut yourself any slack. Just like you would push a bottle of poison away from you if offered, do the same for anxiety. Once you have pushed the poison of anxiety away it is no longer your business to think about it. When our Father says He will take care of something, the last thing we need to do is keep checking up on the problem. He is reliable and does not need to be held accountable by man.

Once the burden is off of your hands you can now trust the God who has proven Himself trustworthy. This will build faith and hope. Faith will help you to be able to trust Him more and hope will get you through the times where it seems like the odds are against you. The hope of God will fill you with all joy and peace through the power of the Holy Ghost (Romans 15:13) and with Him on your side it will soon be impossible for you to fear (Psalm 118:6). Man is no match for the God who created the universe. Fix your heart on these principles and also make a conscious effort to RESIST the devil. He has fiery darts personalized for every single one of us that target your lusts and evil passions. If you resist him, he will flee (James 4:7). God promises that if you are undefiled and walk in His ways that you will be blessed (Psalm 119:1). Call upon His name when you are in distress (Psalm 118:5) and learn to trust in His ability and desire to rescue you. No giant is too big for Him to slay and nothing will stand in the way of Him and His love for you. Putting trust in man will eventually fail you and trusting in ourselves is just the same but remember this...the horse may be prepared for the day of battle but VICTORY LIES IN THE LORD!

> The horse is prepared against the day of battle: but victory **(or safety)** is of the LORD. - Proverbs 21:31 (commentary added)

FEAR ⊕F THE L⊕RD

Now that we have established a practical way to develop trust in The Lord we can move on to a solemn and essential topic...the fear of The Lord. Now before we unpack the fear of The Lord let us lay some groundwork. Would you like to know the whole duty of man on this earth? Ecclesiastes sums up this weighty question with one mere sentence. "Fear God, and keep His commandments: for this is the whole duty of man (Ecclesiastes 12:13). Simple enough right? What about His commandments? Jesus gave us a great starting point for those as well when He said "Thou shalt love The Lord thy God with all thy heart, and with all thy soul, and with all thy mind." and "Thou shalt love thy neighbor as thyself." We must acknowledge our sin and turn from it (repentance) to be forgiven. What is sin? It is a transgression of God's law (1 John 3:4).

> Let us hear the conclusion of the whole matter: Fear God, and keep his commandments: for this is the whole duty of man. - Ecclesiastes 12:13

Master, which is the great commandment in the law? Jesus said unto him, Thou shalt love the Lord thy God with all thy heart, and with all thy soul, and with all thy mind. This is the first and great commandment. And the second is like unto it, Thou shalt love thy neighbor as thyself. - Matthew 22:36-39

If we confess our sins, he is faithful and just to forgive us our sins, and to cleanse us from all unrighteousness. - 1 John 1:9

Whosoever committeth sin transgresseth also the law: for sin is the transgression of the law. - 1 John 3:4

With this foundation, we have some of the basics laid out for us and can now move onto a deeper principle. The fear of The Lord is a requirement for the Knights in Yahweh's Army. It is not as simple as just being "scared" of God. We know Him to be a kind and loving Father whose mercies endure forever (Psalm 136:1). First, we must examine the different ways the Bible uses the word fear.

HEBREW:
Yare' - fear, be afraid
(Strong's Concordance number 3372)
Yare' - fearing; morally, reverent -- afraid, fear (-ful).
(Strong's Concordance number 3373)
Yirah - a fear
(Strong's Concordance number 3374)

GREEK:
Phobéō - to fear, withdraw (flee) from, avoid
(Strong's Concordance number 5399)
Phobos - panic flight, fear, the causing of fear, terror
(Strong's Concordance number 5401)

From these definitions we gather that fear can mean many things including; being afraid, fleeing from, panic, terror, and morally reverent. We can begin to relate this fear to the example I am about to provide. This example is in no way on the same level as this concept but it will have to do for now. When you are riding a horse, you are aware that this thousand-pound animal could crush you were he to fall on you. You are aware that if the beast decided it no longer wanted you on its back that there would be a good chance, he could just buck you off. If you were on a normal tempered horse you would not fear that the horse was out to get you. You would just be aware of the power of the steed and you would hopefully take on an attitude of respect. Now, let's take this example back to the Bible. We should have a feeling of not only respect but a deep feeling of awestruck reverence and awareness at His majesty and power. The only thing we should be terrified of is going against His laws and offending Him. We should also fear His wrath and judgment were we to be set against Him. Being set against The Lord not only endangers your earthly life but more importantly your eternal soul! There is no other true reason to fear than that.

Fear of The Lord is *submission* to His royal will. It also denotes respect for His word and His Son. By choosing to fear Him you are also choosing to respect and revere His word. When you respect and revere His word you lose the luxury of being able to disagree with what it says no matter what you think about it or how it makes you feel. Who are you to disagree with the King? What place does a sword have to disagree with the hand that wields it? We are imperfect vessels who have all sinned standing before a perfect sinless God. There is no room for disputing the King yet only enough room for humbly asking for Him to deepen our understanding or keep us faithful while He chooses to make us wait.

We have all sinned.

For all have sinned, and come short of the glory of God
- Romans 3:23

Yet, our God has NOT sinned.

> For we have not an high priest which cannot be touched
> with the feeling of our infirmities; but was in all points
> tempted like as we are, yet **without sin**. - Hebrews 4:15
> (emphasis added)

Therefore, it is not up to the sinner to question the sinless God.

> So when they continued asking him, he lifted up
> himself, and said unto them, He that is without sin
> among you, let him first cast a stone at her. - John 8:7

Whatever the King says goes and if you disagree then you can easily identify it as user error. How many times have people given up the faith because they seemingly couldn't find answers to burning questions? When asking about the "sons of God" in a church I remember the pastor giving me the same old, tired and utterly false "Sethite View." He tried to tell me that the sons of God that showed up in Genesis 6 and mated with female women to create giants were just men from the line of Seth that mated with the evil women of the line of Cain and were not angels. I had already known that "bene ha Elohim" was used to refer specifically to angels in the book of Job so when he told me this, I was bothered that a so-called "man of God" could take such a weak and easily disproved stance. What made it worse was when he made a joke of the whole conversation the following Sunday in front of the whole flock.

When churches fail to study the scriptures to prove them true like the Bereans did, they also fail to answer many questions that the people of God have. Topics like aliens, demons, gap theory, and God's divine council are rarely ever spoken on or studied by your typical pastor. These things may seem trivial to some but to others they are the major roadblock standing between them and their faith in God. These

Resist tempation, Sin, Addiction

questions *do* have answers and information on them within the Bible. The lack of research given to certain areas have produced "one size fits all", neatly packaged answers like; "Everything's a demon" and "Just trust God". Here's something for those pastors giving those packaged answers. Just say you don't know. Honesty is a virtue discussed many times throughout the Bible you hold so dear.

Back to the topic at hand. In our holy scriptures, we are granted many things if we decide to fear The Lord. This right placed fear is a fountain of life (Proverbs 14:27) and it becomes a place of refuge to those who trust in Him (Proverbs 14:26). If we walk in all His ways, love Him, and serve Him with all of our heart and soul (Deuteronomy 10:12) we will have his unfailing mercy resting upon our lives (Luke 1:50). We will have the beginnings of wisdom, good understanding, (Psalm 111:10) and will replace the fear of man and the fear of worldly matters with the correct fear. Evil will not visit us while we are under His care (Proverbs 19:23) and if evil tries then we will be quick to depart from it (Proverbs 3:7).

Prayer againist

However, if we choose to be wise in our own eyes (Proverbs 3:7) we will become arrogant, prideful, (Proverbs 8:13) and be subject to falling into the snares of the enemy (Proverbs 14:27). It is my belief that we can all come into agreement in saying that it is a fearful thing to fall into the hands of the living God (Hebrews 10:31).

It is a fearful thing to fall into the hands of the living God.
- Hebrews 10:31

DEPENDENCE ON THE SHEPHERD

Trust, Trust, Trust

It goes without saying that the sheep are dependent on their shepherd. They rely on their shepherd for direction and protection. They rely on the shepherd's ability to feed them and keep them. In that same way we are to rely on our Shepherd for wisdom (James 1:5) and to direct our steps as we navigate this side of eternity (Proverbs 3:5-6). We need to run full force into His arms and hold nothing back in our hearts when we give our trust to Him. His timing is not our own and He gives us what we need in due season (Psalm 104:27). He promises to hold our hand and help us while He takes away our fear (Isaiah 41:13). We cast all worry aside because we know that He is reliable and dependable (Philippians 4:6) and that no temptation will take us that is uncommon to us (1 Corinthians 10:13) or that we cannot overcome through his son Yeshua who was tempted in every way we have been but did not sin (Hebrews 4:15). Yeshua becomes our escape from troubles as a good shepherd should. He asks us to let our requests be known to Him (Philippians 4:6) while simultaneously telling us that His thoughts of us are thoughts of peace and not evil (Jeremiah 29:11).

In this life we will have many afflictions and becoming a believer does not exempt you from pain yet The Lord will deliver us out of them all (Psalm 34:19). We serve a Shepherd who never grows weary or faint (Isaiah 40:28-29) as He dwells around those with a humble spirit to revive our spirit in times of need (Isaiah 57:15). He proves Himself dependable by not being a trickster god like some pagans serve who come like a thief to steal, kill and destroy (John 10:10) but instead gives good and perfect gifts from above (James 1:17). His Spirit raised Yeshua from the dead and as a believer, His Spirit dwells inside of us (Romans 8:11) to lead us into all truth and understanding (John 16:13).

Now, what can we do to start learning how to depend on the Father and lean not unto our own understanding?

Here are some starting points:

⊕ **Pray** - Philippians 4:6 tells us to let our requests be known to Him. Developing a strong and growing prayer life will open the lines between us and Him and allow us to communicate and in turn, start to depend on Him.

⊕ **Read the Word** - 2 Timothy 3:16-17 tells us that ALL scripture is inspired by God and profitable for reproof, correction, and instruction in all righteousness.

[handwritten: Be Doers Prayer Big Issue Big time]

⊕ **Act out the Word to the best of your abilities** - James 1:22-25 tells us to be *doers* of the word and not just *hearers*. It tells us that upon doing this we will be blessed in what we do.

We know Father God is a loving and protective Father and He always wishes the best for us. This does not mean that you can put your hand in a furnace because you say "I know God will protect me." This is folly and God gave you a little something called common sense. Do not provoke your Father with stupidity.

Just like a child who is dependent on their mother or a sheep who is dependent on the shepherd we must be dependent on Yahweh. Never straying too far from His sight. If a child strays too far from the sight of the adult, she runs the risk of getting hurt or even kidnapped. If a sheep strays too far from the shepherd it also runs the risk of being hurt or even eaten. Like a prodigal son returning to his father, a sheep who has hurt itself while wandering becomes beaten and bruised. They are sad and hurt as they finally make their way back to the shepherd who receives them with open arms. He takes the sheep and while it is healing, he carries it on the back of his neck. The sheep heals but still walks with a limp that serves as a reminder to never walk too far from the shepherd again. Don't learn the hard way, my friends. Stay close to your shepherd and learn to depend on him for everything.

In summary, trust The Lord who first called you to himself and extended an olive branch of salvation to you while you were still a filthy sinner. Fear The Lord with a holy reverence knowing that He is the creator of the universe who breathed life into your dead lungs. Depend on The Lord as your only source of truth and guidance while navigating this fallen kingdom. These three concepts will set ourselves up with a good start down the path of righteousness.

THE SHIELD OF FAITH

*Above all, taking the shield of faith, wherewith ye shall
be able to quench all the fiery darts of the wicked. -
Ephesians 6:16*

N ow that we have learned about trusting The Lord, fearing Him, and also depending on Him, you are now granted your next piece of equipment which is the Shield of Faith. A must-have in every knight's armory is the shield. They vary in sizes from a small plate sized buckler to a door sized roman *Scutum*. For our purposes, we are speaking of the bigger shield used to protect the whole body. This is exactly what we need to block the flaming aerial attacks of the evil one and his troops of darkness. He will be throwing javelin or spear-like darts at you throughout your walk. They are not intended to kill you but they *will* if you let them get that far. Rather, they are intended to take you off track or slow you down from a distance as you charge toward the enemy for close quarters combat. These javelins can cause anxiety, doubt, uncertainty, discouragement, and disappointment. You are called to take up the shield of faith but also to raise it above your head to stop the arrows and javelins from raining down an onslaught of attacks. Sounds simple enough but even the best warriors can let some of these darts through their guards and when they do the effects can be devastating. We have all had scenarios where we were about to make a big decision and God was seemingly silent (even though He gave us the 66 books of the Bible...doesn't seem so silent but I digress). We went to make the decision but didn't want to go through with it because we were unsure if it was His will or not when all of a sudden, BOOM! Arrows of anxiety and spears of uncertainty and doubt are hurled at us. We become paralyzed and are unable to move in faith. This is not to discourage waiting on God because we know we are told to wait on Him. We should always keep an eye out for signals from His

Holy Spirit. For me personally, there have been times where He has wanted me to move in faith before He got too involved in my choices.

After being assaulted with the enemy's attack we start to feel helpless and start to doubt several truths that we have come to know. One of the worst things that can happen is when we look at how bad the *circumstances* are instead of looking at how faithful our *Father* is. As far as I'm concerned, circumstances are only a small percentage of a situation. They are the hurdle that God will lead you over if you are totally dependent on Him like we learned to be. The amazing thing about the shield of faith is that it is not really *our* faith that it represents. We have read the verses about God being our shield and our buckler, right? Now you see where this applies! The Shield of Faith is the shield of God's faithfulness, ready to protect us from the attacks of the enemy!

> **The Lord is my strength and my shield**; my heart trusted in him, and I am helped: therefore my heart greatly rejoiceth; and with my song will I praise him. - Psalm 28:7 (emphasis added)

> But thou, **O LORD, art a shield for me**; my glory, and the lifter up of mine head. - Psalm 3:3 (emphasis added)

God offered us salvation freely without work of our own and the Shield of Faith is the same situation. Faith is freely given by the Father for us to use and walk in as His people. Use this shield to protect your spiritual body from the enemy's attacks and keep pushing on! The enemy's goal is to achieve one or both of these two things:

1. To get you to force the hand of God and rush His plans for you by trying to take them into your own hands

1. To remove you altogether from the path He has set for you to walk.

The enemy will discourage you to the point where you will not want to walk in God's will or at the very least think yourself unworthy to walk in it. Both strategies remove you from the fight. If Satan can induce stress, anxiety, or panic to get you to try to override God's timing, he will. Don't fall victim to this. Pray and receive the calm during the storm like Jesus did when it was raging all around Him. Everyone in the boat during the storm was giving in to worry, fear, and panic but Jesus instead gave in to the joy and peace of His Father and launched His counterattack. The most effective mindset on the battlefield is the mindset of calmness. Not acting in haste (Proverbs 19:2) but rather keeping a calm mind that is rooted in the truths of God's Word.

> And he said to them, "Why are you afraid, O you of little faith?" Then he rose and rebuked the winds and the sea, and there was a great calm. 27 And the men marveled, saying, "What sort of man is this that even winds and sea obey him?" - Matthew 8:26-27

Every believer will go through these trials and tribulations but do not for one second feel sorry for yourself. There is nothing that is afflicting you that is abnormal to humankind and there is nothing that is thrust upon the believer that is beyond his or her limits. The Lord always provides a way out (1 Corinthians 10:13). Even Lord Yeshua was tested and tried by the enemy so He knows what it is like and knows what we are going through (Hebrews 2:18). Grab that Shield of Faith and hold it strong, warrior!

> There hath no temptation taken you but such as is common to man: but God is faithful, who will not suffer you to be tempted above that ye are able; but will with the temptation also make a way to escape, that ye may be able to bear it. - 1 Corinthians 10:13

> For in that he himself hath suffered being tempted, he is able to succor them that are tempted. - Hebrews 2:18

CHAPTER 12
THE COUNTERFEIT LAMB

"Alright friends. We require a great move of God. God WANTS to bless you. He told me that He has millions of dollars in the storehouses of heaven that He is just waiting to bless all you fine people with. I asked him "Father why wait, couldn't you just bless these people now? My heart is oh so sore seeing them oh so poor!" You know what He told me, folks? I said do you know what He told me? He said.... hold on let me wipe these tears away...okay good...He said that before He blesses you, fine people, He needs to be blessed first. He told me that he needs you to prove your faith by giving Him your treasures because where your treasure is, that is where your heart is folks. The Israelites gave their gold to God and He blessed them, now please lets out give God! You can call this toll-free number to start this great act of faith. Also here is a direct link to my personal PayThisPastor account. Thank you and God bless!

For the second part of the dichotomy, The Lamb, can you guess the counterfeit? It's not just a False Lamb. it is also a Wolf! We've all seen those megachurch televangelist types who tell you to make a seed offering of $1000 dollars so that God will bless you. Disgusting. What about this one, "God told me I need a jumbo jet and it's up to all of you to show your faith and donate". One would think there is a special spot in hell for people who use God to steal from others. Don't get me wrong, there is nothing inherently wrong with a megachurch but I think you are getting the picture I am painting. These men and women are vile wolves at the gates. Even worse than that: *cowardly* wolves disguising themselves as sheep so they can devour the flock.

The evil one and his hounds will come and perform the act of "*metaschématizó*" to "transform" into whatever face you believe rather than their own. Like a wolf wearing a wool coat, they transform into something seemingly pure and good when in reality they are out for blood.

Metaschématizó - is transformed

And no marvel; for Satan himself is transformed (Metaschématizó) into an angel of light. - 2 Corinthians 11:14

He shows up in our quintain (camp) transformed into an angel of light ready to give his dark blessing to those easily fooled. He also has been known to show up to God's Warrior-Priests through his many false prophets, which come to you in sheep's clothing, but inwardly they are ravening wolves. (Matthew 7:15)

Beware of false prophets, which come to you in sheep's clothing, but inwardly they are ravening wolves. - Matthew 7:15

When speaking of these foul knaves it is only appropriate to expose their evil works and show their battle plan to the remnant. Before I list some of the traits of the wolf, I must touch on one other facet of this mindset. Even if we may not be acting as a Wolf, we may still be acting as a False Sheep. Some of the traits are the same between the two however they are sometimes acted out in different ways. For example, The Wolf will show false humility by lying and pretending to be humble, whereas the False Sheep may have a self-defeated mindset that is passed off as humility. Now that we have established the two sub-categories within this Counterfeit Lamb topic, we shall now touch on several ways these two parts exhibit counterfeit traits.

THE COUNTERFEIT LAMB MINDSET

FALSE HUMILITY

WOLF TRAITS   *Prayer of against pride*

⊕ Fakes humility to come off humble but in reality, has a proud heart and proud feelings towards a topic that they don't care to correct.

⊕ Treats people differently based on what they can gain or hide from them.

⊕ Uses humility as a means of manipulation.

FALSE SHEEP TRAITS

⊕ Low self-image and self-esteem.

⊕ Treats people differently based on fear of them or their opinions.

⊕ Worried about others' opinions and what they may think.

⊕ People-pleaser.

⊕ Self-deprecating.

⊕ Weak, timid, and fearful.

FALSE MEEKNESS

WOLF TRAITS

⊕ Unable to show strength or power due to being outmatched so they act as if they are meek (their heart is not in a place of meekness because if they were not outmatched, they would not hold back their strength)

FALSE SHEEP TRAITS

⊕ Terrified to fight back and so weak that they always appear meek (weakness and choosing to be meek are separate issues all to themselves)

FALSE GENTLENESS

WOLF TRAITS

⊕ Pretends to be gentle as a form of manipulation

⊕ Pretends to be gentle as a form of weakness (similar to their behavior on false humility)

FALSE SHEEP TRAITS

⊕ Acts gently out of fear and weakness (similar to their behavior on false meekness)

FALSE PURITY

WOLF TRAITS

⊕ Hasn't come across the opportunity to choose purity over impurity but would choose impurity given the chance yet they come off as pure for the time being

FALSE SHEEP TRAITS

⊕ Surprisingly, the same as the wolf's behavior on this one

Wolves are covetous after the opinions of men and seek to portray themselves as holier than thou. Here is a biblical example of a wolf displaying false humility directly from the holy writ:

> And when thou prayest, thou shalt not be as the hypocrites. Are: for they love to pray standing in the synagogues and in the corners of the streets, that they may be seen of men. - Matthew 6:5

When you seek counterfeit traits and the approval of men you have already received your reward. You have nullified any reward in heaven for your feigned piety. Don't be like this. No one likes it and neither does God.

One of the reasons God allowed the Tree of the Knowledge of Good and Evil to be in the garden was to provide a choice for Adam and Eve. There is no true obedience unless the option to choose disobedience exists. Let's say a man has abstained from sexual intercourse for his whole life but in his heart, he knew that if the opportunity arose to sleep with a beautiful woman, he would take it. Was he really pure or was it false purity? Let's say a man was threatened by a much bigger man over something petty and he chose not to fight back but if he was stronger than his harasser, he would have knocked him out. That would be false meekness because the only reason why he didn't show his strength was that he was outmatched. If he were truly meek, he would not have fought back even if he were the stronger man. Just as there is no true love without the ability to choose that person.

In some of the examples, I mentioned weakness as a cause for the False Sheep to act out these counterfeit behaviors. I want to address that it is not a slight upon the weak. Weakness is a separate issue that is solved by knowing the truth. In the "How the King Views His Knights" part of our journey we went into detail about our identity in Christ and how knowing the truth is the best way to identify the counterfeit. We are to protect the weak and never shame them. Sometimes when a brother grows weak on the field of battle a little tough love can be the remedy. "Snap out of it! You are called to greatness!" is a much more appropriate way to motivate a brother than to say "You are being pathetic, snap out of it or get left behind!"

The Wolf seeks to bring down others to lift himself up. He seeks to prey on the weak. He seeks to deceive others and to cover up his own sinful tracks. Sometimes in our lives, we can unintentionally become a False Sheep by doing the same. When we try to cover up our sin or minimize its severity we are acting like a Counterfeit Lamb (both Wolf and False Sheep). There is no hiding or covering anything up from our Father in Heaven. Just look at what happened when Adam and Eve tried to hide their sin after defying God's command to abstain from eating off the Tree of the Knowledge of Good and Evil:

> And they heard the voice of the LORD God walking in the garden in the cool of the day: and Adam and his wife hid themselves from the presence of the LORD God amongst the trees of the garden. And the LORD God called unto Adam, and said unto him, Where art thou? And he said, I heard thy voice in the garden, and I was afraid because I was naked; and I hid myself. And he said, Who told thee that thou wast naked? Hast thou eaten of the tree, whereof I commanded thee that thou shouldest not eat? - Genesis 3:8-11

There was no detective work on God's part to uncover Adam and Eve's sin. It was bare before Him just as everything else in all of creation is. There is no hiding from an all-knowing, all-seeing God. Any attempt to do so shall be futile. Hiding sin from humans can be done ...for a time. Just remember all things done in the dark will come to light so you are left with no other option than to deal with your sin head-on.

> For nothing is secret that shall not be made manifest; neither anything hid, that shall not be known and come abroad. - Luke 8:17

Discretion, however, is a different matter. For example, if a brother comes to you confessing a sin and asking for help then it is not your job to expose his sin. Neither is it your job to speak about his sin to others. That falls under the topic of *gossip* and in no way are you righteous for partaking in such. Join me in seeing what the wisdom of the Book of Proverbs says on the matter:

> Discretion shall preserve thee, understanding shall keep thee - Proverbs 2:11

> That thou mayest regard discretion, and that thy lips may keep knowledge. - Proverbs 5:2

> A talebearer revealeth secrets: but he that is of a faithful spirit concealeth the matter. - Proverbs 11:13

> He that covereth a transgression seeketh love; but he that repeateth a matter separateth very friends. - Proverbs 17:9

When it comes down to it, honesty before our King is the only route we have to take. If we cannot be honest in front of men, we are practicing dishonesty, which will eventually lead to dishonesty with our Father. We all sin and fall short of the glory of God so hiding it will only delay the correcting of it. Discretion should still be practiced when helping a loved one through their sin.

BU+ I'M A G⊕⊕D PERS⊕N!

Our last stop in the Counterfeit Lamb study is a look at a person we have all met many times in our lives. I call them the "Good Person." They gamble their entire salvation on how good they think they are. They fail to realize that no one person on this planet is truly righteous.

> As it is written, There is none righteous, no, not one -
> Romans 3:10

They assume the God of Heaven will let them spend eternity with Him when they never took the time to read His Word that He wrote to us. Let me ask you this: if a known criminal walked up to you off of the street and asked to live in your house for a week what would you say? He doesn't look too dangerous. He just looks like a normal man. What would you do? You don't know this man from Adam and have never seen him before in your life. Now it is safe to assume you would say "No, you cannot live with me because I don't know who you are." Now what if that man said "Wait, it's okay because I'm a good person!" That answer wouldn't hold up too well when you have to decide who gets to be around your family. It is similar to how some people act toward God. They want to live and spend eternity with a God they have never met, never talked to, or never even learned about.

If people who say they will get into Heaven based on them being a "good person" even bothered to read their Bible, they would know that we are not saved by works.

> For by grace are ye saved through faith; and that not of yourselves: it is the gift of God: Not of works, lest any man should boast. - Ephesians 2:8-9

It is by the grace of God that we are saved through faith. It is not something that can be earned. If it were something that we could earn then it would be *our* strength that made it happen and not God's. It always breaks my heart when I meet someone who thinks this way because they think that they are fine when in reality they are just as in danger of hell fire as a murderer or a rapist. It is even worse when you encounter people that actually have a pretty good life. Without anything going wrong in their life why would they need religion or faith? At least that is how they view it. Those can be some of the hardest people to reach and it saddens me deeply. The day will come where they will go through trials and tribulation but until that point it is hard to convince someone that a flood is coming when the skies are clear. We must pray for how to reach these people and show them where their assumptions about the God they don't know are actually false and have no basis in fact. This must all be done in love of course.

That sums up the Counterfeit Lamb portion of our study and also draws a conclusion to the Lion and the Lamb dichotomy as a whole. We have already learned so much but we have only scratched the surface. Also, we haven't even uncovered a full set of armor so we can't stop here! It is now time to tackle the dichotomy from where this book gets its namesake...The Warrior and The Priest dichotomy!

CHAPTER 13
THE WARRIOR AND THE PRIEST

The hot sun was waning as the day drew to a close. Joshua stood on the cliff's edge staring out towards the massive walls of Jericho. He was scraping the dirt off of the hilt of his sword thinking about the great weight on his shoulders. He had been given Moses' mantle as leader of Yahweh's people and the task of reclaiming the Promised Land was his. His Lord always reminded him to be strong and courageous but the truth was ... he was scared. He was scared of failing his family, his people, and, most of all, his God.

Often times Caleb would find him late at night standing outside his tent staring off into the stars with a somber look on his face. "Joshua, you mustn't trouble yourself like this. God would not have appointed you as our leader if He did not already know you can succeed." Caleb was like a brother to Joshua and sometimes even like a Father. They would spar when training for battle and more often than naught Caleb would be winning. That is until Joshua became a sore loser and would best Caleb with a barrage of furious strikes and sheer determination. He loved him. "I know what you say is true Caleb. Somehow it doesn't make the weight any less to bear."

This day Caleb was training the young men on his own as Joshua was scouting the areas around Jericho. He sent his men home and was lost in his thoughts watching the hot sun start to set when all of a sudden, he felt a change in the air. He couldn't explain it but it felt like he was no longer alone. "Who goes there?!" Joshua demanded as he snapped his sword into position and turned around on a moment's notice. That's when he saw him.

There was a man walking up the hill. He was wearing a white robe and something about him reminded Joshua of Moses. Whenever Moses would exit the holy of holies his face would glow. This man had that same look. He was wearing white robes that were stained with blood. Joshua thought it odd that the man had no armor on but somehow, he knew that this man was dangerous. Dangerous and very powerful. The drawn sword in the man's hand reinforced that notion.

"Are you for us or for our adversaries?" Joshua called out to the man as he tightened his grip on his sword and stood firm in his warrior's stance. The man silently stared at him before taking a couple more steps then stopping. He was in no rush. He stared at Joshua and his eyes seemed to be made out of fire. Joshua was frozen in place unsure of what to make of this strange man. Then he spoke. "I am for neither. I have come as the Captain of the Hosts of The Lord."

Immediately Joshua fell to knees and his nose touched the dirt. Once he realized who this man was his knee shot to the ground out of his own free will, however, he had a feeling that even if he had not wanted to kneel his knee would have betrayed him and knelt anyways. This man... was no mere man. He was the King of Kings!

The Lord is a man of war: The Lord is his name. -
Exodus 15:3

Here we go! The Warrior and The Priest. Two seemingly opposite mindsets yet both are found in the man or woman of God. The strength of The Warrior and the holiness of The Priest. One paves his way with a sword and a battle cry. The other tears down the spiritual realm and heals his allies in prayer. One bears the shield and the other bears the cross. I think you get the picture.

Now why would I write a story about Joshua from the Bible as the introduction to The Warrior and The Priest section? Wasn't he just a warrior and not a priest? True he was a warrior and true he did not have the title of official priest however he was a fighting man of God. This is what I wish for you to understand and grasp. The men and women of God are nothing without their faith.

Joshua was the right-hand man of Moses. When Moses was leading God's people, Joshua was by his side learning from him. He even went up to the mountain of God *with* Moses! He learned all that he could and was a *servant* to Moses before he was allowed to become a *leader* of God's people.

One thing that always struck me as fascinating about Joshua is when Moses went into the tent to meet with the presence of God, he asked Joshua to go with him. Not only did Joshua get to sit in the very presence of God but when Moses left, he got to stay behind! This is one of those gems I feel like the Bible has lit up for me personally. What was he doing in there? We may never know but I sure hope we get to find out in eternity.

Some of us do lean to one side more than the other when it comes to being a warrior or a priest but to tip the scales too much in one direction will make us one dimensional in our growth. To ignore one side is to do yourself a disservice. This does not mean that you may not be gifted more in one area over another. For example, Moses led with a staff and when it came time for Joshua to take over, Joshua led with a spear. I would say that Moses was slightly more priest and

Joshua was slightly more warrior. The same goes for David and his son Solomon. David was a man of war, which counted him out from building the temple, yet he wrote many beautiful psalms. Solomon was not a man of war and was allowed to build God's holy temple on earth. Ultimately, it is up to our Father in Heaven to determine the balance He wants each of us to have.

So back to the subject at hand. How was Joshua a warrior and a priest? We can start by his relationship with the Living God. We already talked about how he was face to face with Father God. He was also personally commissioned by God to lead His people after Moses (Joshua 1:2-9). Through God's power and Joshua's instruction, the Israelites cross the Jorden River on dry land, only after sanctifying themselves. By doing this he showed that he had knowledge and a reverence for the Living God as a true priest should. Joshua also set up memorial stones to always remember what God had done for them at the Jordan and told the Israelites to have their children hear the story when they asked what the stones were for (Joshua 4:5-7). If that wasn't enough to show you that Joshua was a holy man of God then what about when he prayed to the Father for the sun to stand still and how God actually listened to him (Joshua 10:12-13)? The Bible even says that this is the only time like this where God heeded the voice of a man! I rest my case.

This next point will be a no brainer but it definitely deserves a look. Joshua of the Bible was a *warrior*. This man and his warriors put their feet on the necks of five kings from the surrounding areas while telling his people, "Fear not, nor be dismayed, be strong and of good courage: for thus shall The Lord do to all your enemies against whom ye fight." He then slashed their necks and hung them from trees (Joshua 10:25-26)! Joshua was tasked with clearing out the Promised Land of all Nephilim men, women, children, and all those who interbred with them. He only suffered defeat when Achan plundered items that he wasn't supposed to and removed God's protection from the people of Israel. Other than that, the man was a decorated warrior. If reading about Joshua doesn't pump you up than I doubt anything will! Let's move on and learn about The Warrior.

CHAPTER 14
THE WARRIOR

The Warrior's Fire

I have known nothing but fighting
I have trained years for this
My hands are covered in blood and my heart is heavy
My joints are aching and my vision is blurred
My body is failing but my spirit is strong
My flesh is in subjection to my spirit and
My spirit drives me on
I want to quit but I know I cannot
I think of surrender but quickly rebuke it
I have fought for years with no end in sight
I feel the grass in my hands as I pick myself up off the floor
I grab my side and feel wet blood dripping from my wound
My pain tells me to stop but my heart tells me I cannot
Everything in me wants to give up and die
But I cannot
My life is not my own

I am not fighting for me
I am fighting for my countrymen
I am fighting for my family
I am fighting for my GOD
I am the Warrior

Blessed be the Lord my strength which teacheth my
hands to war, and my fingers to fight - Psalm 144:1

The Lord our God is, in fact, a man of war (Exodus 15:3). He is many things; loving, kind, forgiving, just, and a warrior. These things do not contradict one another. Each has its time and place. There is no separating the warrior from our Lord. Yeshua will return as Messiah ben David, the Lion of the tribe of Judah, and bring war to the evil forces on the earth in the last days. He returns with eyes of flaming fire, wielding a sword, and wearing blood-stained robes. This man is a warrior through and through.

> Now I saw heaven opened, and behold, a white horse. And He who sat on him was called Faithful and True, and in righteousness, He judges and makes war. 12 His eyes were like a flame of fire, and on His head were many crowns. - Revelation 19:11-12

Our King is referred to as the "Lord of Hosts" many times throughout scriptures. This means that He is the commander of the hosts (armies) of Heaven. Legions of angel armies are at His beck and call. Elisha prayed that the eyes of the servant with him would be open to see the reinforcement of heavenly horses and chariots they had from Yahweh.

> And Elisha prayed, and said, Lord, I pray thee, open his eyes, that he may see. And the Lord opened the eyes of the young man; and he saw: and, behold, the mountain was full of horses and chariots of fire round about Elisha. - 2 Kings 6:17

As men and women made in His image, we too are warriors, whether it be physical warfare or spiritual warfare, The Lord teaches us how to participate in both. The Lord will go forth into battle as a warrior and arouse His zeal while shouting a tremendous war cry as He defeats His enemies (Isaiah 42:13). He loathes arrogance and destroys whole cities packed with citadels because of it (Amos 6:8). His touch alone melts the land and tramples on the high places of other so-called gods (Amos 9:5, 4:13). He is known by His enemies as a terrifying, awe-inspiring dread champion (Jeremiah 20:11) who breaks through breach after breach and runs at His foes (Job 16:14). His persecutors will never prevail and will only find shame on the battlefield. They will seek peace but it will be too late and they will only find destruction (Ezekiel 7:25). His brave warriors have no fear, save for the fear of The Lord, and offer their bodies as a living sacrifice (Romans 12:1) in battle because they know that while the enemy can take their lives, they can never take their souls (Matthew 10:28)! They are made more than conquerors through the love of their Commander (Romans 8:37).

When you fight on the side of Yahweh you hear His thundering voice throughout the ranks of His great armies. He makes His warriors strong if they carry out His will and no enemy can endure His great day (Joel 2:11). We can rest easy knowing that in His perfect will we will not die before our appointed time. We strive to never be outside of His protective perimeter. Footman upon footman can be heard crying out "The Lord is in our midst, the great victorious warrior!" (Zephaniah 3:17). He brings justice to those who have been wronged (James 5:4) and defends the helpless. Blood that has been shed by evil men calls out from the ground for Him to exact his righteous fury upon the culprits (Genesis 4:10). When we go out into battle and are surrounded by horses and chariots that far surpass our own numbers, we will NOT be afraid, for our God is with us and THEY are the ones who are outnumbered (Deuteronomy 20:1-4)! Now let us learn some of the traits of the warrior mindset.

Then David said to the Philistine, "You come to me with a sword, a spear, and a javelin, but I come to you in the name of the LORD of hosts, the God of the armies of Israel, whom you have taunted. - 1 Samuel 17:45

THE WARRIOR MINDSET

⊕ **Strength** - The warrior's strength is given to him and demanded of him from his heavenly Father.

I can do all things through Christ which strengtheneth me. - Philippians 4:13

Have not I commanded thee? Be strong and of a good courage; be not afraid, neither be thou dismayed: for the Lord thy God is with thee whithersoever thou goest. - Joshua 1:9

⊕ **Discipline** - The warrior needs discipline to continue in his training and to maintain control over his warrior spirit. The Lord is happy to oblige willing apprentices.

Be ye strong therefore, and let not your hands be weak: for your work shall be rewarded. - 2 Chronicles 15:7

He that hath no rule over his own spirit is like a city that is broken down, and without walls. - Proverbs 25:28

⊕ **Bravery** - Bravery is a must for the warrior who will face many daunting and terrifying circumstances where he must continue forward despite his circumstances. The odds matter little when God is your defender.

The wicked flee when no man pursueth: but the righteous are bold as a lion. - Proverbs 28:1

For God hath not given us the spirit of fear; but of power, and of love, and of a sound mind. - 2 Timothy 1:7

⊕ **Relentlessness** - The warrior never quits and never surrenders. He knows his mission is only complete when his life is over and he will keep pressing towards the finish line.

And let us not be weary in well doing: for in due season we shall reap, if we faint not. - Galatians 6:9

Rejoicing in hope; patient in tribulation; continuing instant in prayer - Romans 12:12

⊕ **Confidence** - The warrior's confidence comes from his heavenly Father and not from himself. Therefore, he has a never-ending supply since his God is all powerful.

For the LORD shall be thy confidence, and shall keep thy foot from being taken. - Proverbs 3:26

Fear thou not; for I am with thee: be not dismayed; for I am thy God: I will strengthen thee; yea, I will help thee; yea, I will uphold thee with the right hand of my righteousness. - Isaiah 41:10

Not that we are sufficient of ourselves to think anything as of ourselves; but our sufficiency is of God - 2 Corinthians 3:5

⊕ **Patience** - The warrior knows when to strike and when to restrain. He knows when it is best to wait and not jump into action. Consulting The Lord in prayer before decisions is a must.

Rest in the LORD, and wait patiently for him: fret not thyself because of him who prospereth in his way, because of the man who bringeth wicked devices to pass. - Psalms 37:7-9

Be not hasty in thy spirit to be angry: for anger resteth in the bosom of fools. - Ecclesiastes 7:9

WAR IS UP⊕N US

We live in the last days. The final hour. Anyone who is paying attention can see the signs of men calling good evil and evil good (Isaiah 5:20). There are famines, pestilences, wars, rumors of wars, and earthquakes in diverse place. There have even been reports of labs in the United Kingdom and China creating animal-human hybrids and further plunging us right into the "days of Noah" (Matthew 24:37-39). The reports said that they destroyed over two hundred animal-human hybrid semi-sentient embryos and my first thought upon hearing this was "If they are coming out and saying publicly that they have this technology then the technology they really have must far surpass this" and also "If they threw away two hundred I wonder how many they kept and how far they have grown them."

The days of Noah were marked with Watcher angels coming to Earth and wreaking havoc, performing DNA manipulation to create hybrids and other unsanctioned creations like giants, propagating transhumanism, promising longer life spans, conducting abortions and a myriad of other rebellious acts against the God of the Bible. Now let us turn to the great-grandfather of Noah, Enoch. I must first say that obviously no text carries the same weight as the inherent, inspired and authoritative word of God. However, Enoch is referenced several times in scripture (Luke 3:37, Hebrews 11:5, Jude 1:14-15) and is also a part of the Ethiopian canon. I highly encourage you to form your own opinion of the validity of the book of Enoch and I will not rob you of that journey by forcing my opinions on you. It takes place right before the flood which would land it right in the aforementioned days of Noah and it has some interesting things to say about this generation. Within the first couple verses, Enoch states that he saw a vision of the Holy One in the heavens shown to him by the angels and that the vision was not for his generation but for a remote one which is to come (Enoch 2). The book has many references to Yeshua's second coming and for me personally, I believe these two reasons are why the book has been hidden and shrouded from the public eye for millennia.

Our vile nation now has Drag Queen story time in public libraries where homosexual men and convicted sex offenders have been entertaining children. What kind of sick Moloch worshippers subject their children to this?! Enoch 98:2 states "men shall put on more adornments than a woman and more colored garments than a virgin" and shall be found "wanting in doctrine and wisdom" before their spirits are "cast into the furnace of fire." This is scary! The reason why I bring the book of Enoch into this discussion is because of how spot on the prophecy is speaking of our day. Not a future day but THIS VERY DAY!

> For ye, men shall put on more adornments than a woman, And coloured garments more than a virgin - Enoch 98:2

What's even more chilling to read is what Enoch says about *abortion*. Now with New York approving abortion up until the third trimester recently and debates raging for even "after birth abortions", or MURDER as I call it, our land is mirroring an ancient prophecy given in Enoch. And in case you were wondering about the origins of abortions, it mentions that too!

> And barrenness has not been given to the woman, but on **account of the deeds of her own hands**, she dies without children. - Enoch 98:5 (emphasis added)

And the fifth was named Kasdeja: this is he who showed the children of men all the wicked smitings of spirits and demons, and the **smitings of the embryo in the womb, that it may pass away** [...] - Enoch 69:12 (emphasis added)

The point of all of this is to prove to you that we are in an all-out war with the enemies of our souls. Not only are they attacking our men and women but now they are using our own women to destroy our children worse than ever before. Imagine all of the blood crying out from the ground across America for justice from the Father, which He will bring in the form of a deluge of fire. Our Lord does NOT bear the sword in vain (Romans 13:4). We as Christians need to take on the Warrior-Priest Mindset and wage war against evil laws and policies by exposing them, praying for those in office, and supporting those who uphold biblical Christian values.

Think not that I am come to send peace on earth: I came not to send peace, but a sword. - Matthew 10:34

CHAPTER 15
KNOW THY ENEMY

For we wrestle not against flesh and blood, but against
principalities, against powers, against the rulers of the
darkness of this world, against spiritual wickedness in
high places. - Ephesians 6:12

If you don't believe that your enemies exist then how can you fight them? The same goes for the spiritual realm and the forces within it. From the spiritual realm, these forces can mount attacks in the physical realm. We are all aware of the physical war that rages around us whether it be in the doctor's chairs against our unborn children or whether it be on the actual field of battle fought with weapons of modern warfare. However, Ephesians tells us that the heart of the battle lies is in the spiritual realm. When Peter tried to stop Jesus from giving his life, there was a supernatural force acting behind Peter to deceive him into influencing Jesus to alter His plan for salvation (Matthew

16:22-23). Yeshua's response was to rebuke him and also the spiritual force *behind* him which I believe was in fact, Satan.

> Then Peter took him, and began to rebuke him, saying, Be it far from thee, Lord: this shall not be unto thee. But he turned, and said unto **Peter, Get thee behind me, Satan**: thou art an offence unto me: for thou savourest not the things that be of God, but those that be of men.
> - Matthew 16:22-23 (emphasis added)

Jesus addresses the spiritual realm which contained the source of the problem. Peter was stopped later in Matthew when Judas and his band of miscreants came to capture Jesus. Again, Peter was inadvertently altering God's spiritual plans for salvation. (Matthew 26). Ephesians, or the Spiritual Warfare Manual as I call it, tells us that our battles in this world are not against flesh and blood but against spiritual forces in high places.

> For we wrestle not against flesh and blood, but against principalities, against powers, against the rulers of the darkness of this world, against spiritual wickedness in high places. - Ephesians 6:12

When the text mentions principalities, powers, rulers of darkness and spiritual wickedness in high places it is referring to fallen angels, demons, and various other spiritual rulers and entities. These have also been referred to as unclean spirits, daemons, or elemental spirits. Fallen angels have also portrayed themselves as great gods in every culture and have been worshipped by the pagans throughout the ages (think Greek pantheon and Egyptian gods). We know that Satan is the "prince of the power of the air" (Ephesians 2:2) and "god of this world" (2 Corinthians 4:4). Ephesians 2 also tells us that he is also the spirit that now works in the children of disobedience!

Wherein in time past ye walked according to the course
of this world, according to the prince of the power of
the air, the spirit that now worketh in the children of
disobedience - Ephesians 2:2

We can also read in Enoch how the spirits of the deceased giants
could not enter into heaven since they were of not of heaven but of
the earth. They were then free to roam the Earth and terrorize the
children of Adam.

And now, the giants, who are produced from the spirits
and flesh, shall be called evil spirits upon the earth, and
on the earth shall be their dwelling. Evil spirits have
proceeded from their bodies; because they are born from
men, and from the holy Watchers is their beginning and
primal origin; they shall be evil spirits on earth, and evil
spirits shall they be called. [As for the spirits of heaven, in
heaven shall be their dwelling, but as for the spirits of the
earth which were born upon the earth, on the earth shall
be their dwelling.] And the spirits of the giants afflict,
oppress, destroy, attack, do battle, and work destruction
on the earth, and cause trouble: they take no food, but
nevertheless hunger and thirst, and cause offences. And
these spirits shall rise up against the children of men and
against the women, because they have proceeded from
them. - Enoch 15:8-12

The spirits of the giants, fallen angels and Satan himself are what we
are up against. We are NO MATCH in the flesh for these entities and it
is only through the power of Yahweh and the name of Jesus that we can

make spiritual war against these forces and defend our family. This lets us know that the flesh and blood humans in front of us are not our real enemy! When a militant atheist is screaming in your face it is not the atheist that is your enemy. It is the lies they have been fed that led them to this point or the pain that they have suffered sometimes at the hands of believers that have turned them against the Most High. The real enemy of our souls will *use* people and work through them to make the war fought on a physical realm instead of where the battle is really at, the spiritual realm. An example of this would be like a man who has been demonized through a trauma that happened in his life. He starts taking drugs to self-medicate and the demon's influence in his life get stronger. Now he pulls a knife on you to rob you. In this example, a series of pain and bad choices have led this man to be under the influence of demons. He is physically manifesting behaviors that stem from the spiritual realm. The Bible doesn't mention "possession" but instead uses the Greek word "*daimonizomai*" which means demonized. Demons cannot "possess" a believer but they can demonize or tempt, lie, encourage anger and bitterness, cloud our judgment, provoke our fears, cause panic, induce depression or despair, or even destroy our relationships with those around us. Evil spirits wish to make you an ineffective knight in God's service and don't care what you believe as long as it's not the truth. Pain and suffering are the tools of the enemy's trade and these spirits can be responsible for causing a great number of mental, physical and spiritual problems such as blindness, madness, or diseases (Matthew 12:22, Mark 5:4,5). Since a demon is a disembodied spirit of a giant it is safe to say that they wish to act out vile sins of the flesh vicariously through influencing a human since they too were once beings of flesh.

There are only three sources of influence for humans and they are the flesh (which is at war with the spirit), demonic influence, and the influence of the Holy Spirit. Whichever you yield to will have a greater influence in your life over the others. If you spend more time in God's word than you do entertaining your flesh then you can expect His influence to be greater and vice versa. Now let us form a plan of attack for dealing with the spiritual battles that lie ahead.

SPIRI+UAL PLAN ⊕F A++ACK

First things first. In this spiritual war, our source of power and protection comes from the Most High God of the Bible, Yahweh. We need to repent of any sin in our lives and remove them from our path. We should be constantly looking for areas where we are not living the way God wants us to and surrender them to Him through prayer. His power and protection are the only things that let us make it through this war when dealing with such spiritual mega-threats. Man was made lower than the angels (Hebrews 2:7) and if a giant is a cross between a man and an angel then we would be a little lower than them as well. Now if these spiritual beings are more powerful than us fleshly beings how do we even stand a chance? Through Yahweh. It is with His holy name that we are permitted to banish these threats and keep His wings of protection over us. In His mercy, He has allowed me personally to use His name to break demonic oppression from myself when I was first becoming a believer and did not yet have a strong relationship with Him. This strategy did not go so well for the Sons of Sceva (Jewish exorcists) who thought they knew the "secret name" of the Jewish God and tried to use it to banish demons without having a relationship with Him (Acts 19:15-16). I believe the difference between what I did and what they did was that I was *becoming* a believer and they were just seeking power.

> And the evil spirit answered and said, Jesus I know, and Paul I know; but who are ye? And the man in whom the evil spirit was leaped on them, and overcame them, and prevailed against them, so that they fled out of that house naked and wounded. - Acts 19:15-16

I believe God gives us mercy and grace by allowing us to use His name to stop a demonic attack when we are new to the faith or inquiring about it. However, I also believe that if someone tries to use the gifts of God without the relationship with Him they will soon find their authority to use His name to be gone. If you are going through a demonic attack whether it be at night in the dark or broad daylight a simple prayer I would say is:

"Leave in Jesus name!"

That's where I started and it worked for me. Now if you were trying to clear the spiritual cobwebs out and further safeguard yourself against openings to attack, I will show you what I personally would pray:

> "Father God, I repent of (whatever sin) and ask for your forgiveness. I thank you that you have made me new and even though I make mistakes I will come to you and not return to my sin. I am sorry and I no longer want to do those sins. I ask that you remove all evil spirits from around me and their influence in my life and you close any doors that may be open to them. I renounce anything I have done that has allowed evil spirits to mess with me. Please reveal any areas in my life that you need me to change and repent of that are not yielded over to you and please give me your Psalms 91 protection. I love you Father God and thank you for everything you have done for me and my family and for always providing for us. In Yeshua's name I pray, amen."

That is just a starting point for me personally and I would suggest taking that prayer and *anything* I say in this book straight to The Lord in prayer and ask Him to reveal His truth and toss out whatever is left.

AN ENEMY IN THE CAMP

Real and effective spiritual warfare is up to the individual believer. You must take care of your own spiritual home as well as your physical home. Evil forces are always looking for an "open door" through which they can have a legal right to attack a believer. They are like a bandit hitching a ride on your carriage and trying to snatch the reigns from the driver's hands. The sad part is that most professing Christians either don't believe in demons or don't give them a second thought. So much for knowing your enemy! There are also people on the opposite side of the spectrum who accuse everything of being demonic, without realizing that their flesh is the culprit many of those times. When it comes to the flesh and to the demonic both areas must be dealt with. Every so often I like to do what I call a "spiritual purge". It is similar to the ancient people removing the leaven (representative of sin) from their house before Passover (1 Corinthians 5:7). What it entails is taking anything that I have that has any occult, demonic, sexual, or overly violent themes in it and throwing it out. Just like in the book of Acts when the Christian converts at Ephesus burned their occult/sorcery books (Acts 19:19).

> Many of them also which used curious arts (**magic arts in ESV**) brought their books together, and burned them before all men: and they counted the price of them, and found it fifty thousand pieces of silver. - Acts 19:19 (commentary added)

Now I don't resell them for a profit because I don't want to be responsible for re-circulating occult or demonic material into the world to then fall into someone else's hands and possibly lead them astray. You need to remove anything that glorifies witchcraft, sex or the occult. Nudity is also very dangerous in that it will not only ruin your view of women but also your relationship with your spouse. It is mental adultery and Jesus specifically spoke out against that.

> But I say unto you, That whosoever looketh on a woman to lust after her hath committed adultery with her already in his heart. - Matthew 5:28

When it comes to magic and the occult, why hang on to the counterfeit when the real miracles are way better. What we also see in the book of Acts is Jesus and His disciples casting out demons from people and healing the sick right before everyone's eyes to reclaim the lives the demons had stolen. This is far better than any cheap demonic parlor trick. Now let us remove all tools of the enemy from our presence. Here is a short list of witchcraft, demonic, magic or occult items that I believe must be removed and destroyed from our lives. I would repent of participating in the works of darkness after the removal and destruction of the following items:

⊕ Harry Potter or any other wizard/warlock/witch materials

⊕ Video games with magic or spell casting (sorcery)

⊕ Spell books or other occult books

⊕ Halloween themed items

⊕ Fortune telling items

⊕ Tarot cards or any other divination items

⊕ New age books or music

⊕ Yoga books or music

⊕ Pornographic or lude items

⊕ Eastern mysticism items

⊕ Any other items from other religions such as talismans, statues, totems, fetishes or voodoo dolls

⊕ Anything that glorifies sorcery, magic, new age, or the occult.

This is by no means an exhaustive list but it is a great place to start removing the influence of the enemy and his roving band of demon sorcerers. In ancient times, sorcery was sometimes used to control powerful entities, to gain information, or even in defense to protect from other less powerful evil spirits. Back then the majority of people seemingly feared these entities and wished to be protected against them. Nowadays people are practically in love with these entities and it shows through various means including music and music videos containing; werewolves, vampires, Satanism, witchcraft, and even cannibalism! There are even "Christian witches" which is the biggest oxymoron I've ever heard of next to "Christian yoga"! Let us finally settle the score for people who still engage in yoga. Here is the definition:

Yoga - a Hindu spiritual and ascetic discipline, a part of which, including breath control, simple meditation, and the adoption of specific bodily postures, is widely practiced for health and relaxation.

Right here we can see that you cannot separate the HINDU Spiritism from the practice of yoga. What is Hinduism you ask? Let's take a look.

Hinduism - a major religious and cultural tradition of South Asia, which developed from Vedic religion.

Hinduism by definition is a straight up other religion! So, yoga is a Hindu spiritual practice and Hinduism is a different religion besides Christianity! What does Yahweh have to say about other religions and the gods in them?

Thou shalt have no other gods before me...Thou shalt not bow down thyself to them, nor serve them: for I the Lord thy God am a jealous God... - Exodus 20:3, 5 (emphasis added)

Now it is settled and anyone reading this who does yoga must repent and stop right now in light of all this information presented. The crazy part is all I did was show how those two words are defined and that's all it took to uncover its spiritually adulterous meaning.

In this day and age, people are using sins that God detests as tools of entertainment! They even influence our young and pack cartoons full of these things. When I was young Harry Potter was the most popular thing out and I even read all the books and watched all the movies (of which I've since repented and tossed out). Now into my adult years, there are more practicing and professing witches on the rise than there are practicing and confessing Christians! We are starting to see the dark fruit from the Harry Potter era and it is sad. When it comes to magic or the occult, they usually always entail supernatural powers drawn from a source other than the God of the Bible or gaining power/knowledge from a supernatural entity other than Yahweh. Think about it, why would you play a game where your character is a warlock and summons demons to do his bidding when you *know* for a fact that God hates that type of behavior?

> Thou shalt not suffer a witch to live. - Exodus 22:18

> And he made his son pass through the fire, practiced witchcraft and used divination, and dealt with mediums and spiritists. He did much evil in the sight of the LORD provoking Him to anger. - 2 Kings 21:6

> And I will cut off sorceries from your hand, and you shall have no more tellers of fortunes - Micah 5:12 ESV

What is even craftier is a video game where you are murdering people and robbing and killing can fall under the same bracket. I would be very careful about which games you allow you or your family to play and never be ignorant of their contents. Also, anything that glorifies any other gods or religious figures should be destroyed. A statue of Odin or a poster with Greek gods on it are both just propaganda of fallen angels and demonstrate their influence on our culture. If you knew what these entities are capable of you would not have pictures of them up in your room. Anyone who has had a demonic attack at night as I have will soon find out that games with demons in them are no longer cute. They no longer entertain when you realize these entities are real and would not waste one moment to maim, kill, or rape you given the chance. Thankfully we can pray in Jesus' name for the attack to cease and they will leave. One time I could barely even mumble the name of our Savior while an entity was holding my mouth shut and putting pressure on my chest yet thanks be to Father that even that mumble of His name stopped the attack. The bottom line is that these things are the enemy's methods of operation and propaganda. A believer should have no fellowship with darkness but instead destroy it.

> And have no fellowship with the unfruitful works of darkness, but rather reprove them. - Ephesians 5:11

> Some trust in chariots, and some in horses: but we will remember the name of the Lord our God - Psalm 20:7

Never be so attached to your favorite movie, game or franchise that you would rather hold on to *that* than to God. Is your love of those things so great that you would rather spit in the face of God and insult Him than to give it up and sacrifice it on the altar? Do you know how many things I've thrown away that I loved at the time and did not want to part with? Tons. This is not to toot my own shofar but rather to show you that I deal with this too from time to time and I have struggled just like you will.

I have given you a view into things that I myself practice. You may have different liberties and convictions than me and that is between you and Yahweh. However, there are many things that are not up to the believer to decide if he or she is okay with it. For instance, God would never be okay with someone watching pornography even if they said that they did not feel convicted about it. I did not write these things down as a fully exhaustive list that everyone must adhere too. I am only sharing with you how I live my life according to what I have researched in the Bible. There are some materials about pagan gods that I have watched as research. Did I sin by doing so? I don't believe so. If I were to watch those materials and long after what those gods can do or started to root for them as my heroes, I believe that would go beyond the point of research. You cannot fool God but you can, however, attempt to fool yourself. Really examine your motives for everything you do and search the scriptures to see if the things that you call "entertainment" are referred to in the Bible as "sins".

Love not the world, neither the things that are in the world. If any man love the world, the love of the Father is not in him. For all that is in the world, the lust of the flesh, and the lust of the eyes, and the pride of life, is not of the Father, but is of the world. And the world passeth away, and the lust thereof: but he that doeth the will of God abideth for ever. - 1 John 2:15-17

CHAPTER 16
THE COUNTERFEIT WARRIOR

The lance broke against Lord Banneck's shield swinging his body backward and almost off of his horse. Lord Banneck hated losing more than anything and he was angry that this young boy of a knight had actually landed a blow upon him. "Good match Lord Banneck!" yelled the boy knight Sir Gallen. "Don't patronize me, boy, let us ride again and this time I shan't hold back!" Lord Banneck raged. They rode to their spots and as the heralds blew their trumpets the two knights charged toward each other once more. Lord Banneck hated losing and he would make sure it wouldn't happen again. He refused to be shamed by this young knight no matter how good he was. The young knight was from the neighboring kingdom and had served in the military. He was renowned as an honorable man and always helped those in need.

Right before they clashed together, Lord Banneck raise his lance and aimed for Sir Gallen's helm instead of his shield. CRACK! The lance snapped off and sent Sir Gallen reeling off of the back of his horse. After a couple of minutes, the knight stood up and called out to Lord Banneck "You raised your lance at the last minute to do me harm! You know that the rules of the tournament do not allow combatants to aim for the helm!"

Lord Banneck had had just about enough of this insolent pup. "You dare call out my honor you green boy! I've heard of your honor and frankly, I'm sick of the tales. It is your skill of blade that concerns me now!" Lord Banneck yelled as he dismounted and drew his sword charging the fallen knight without waiting for him to acknowledge the challenge. Sir Gallen could not stand up in time and only just managed to draw his blade to block the head strike that was about to cave in his great helm. Gasps were heard all through the crowd at such a display of dishonor. Lord Banneck knew it was dishonorable but he was so angry that this boy addressed him in such a way that he saw no other option than to protect his precious pride.

The boy managed to roll to the side of Banneck's wild slashes and finally got his footing. Banneck was swinging like a mad man driven by anger. Sir Gallen had fought men like this before. Gallen was a patient man and was never given to anger. He learned from his father at a young age that a man who controlled his spirit could rule kingdoms. Lord Banneck struck the side of Sir Gallen's arm denting the armor before he could spin away. "Patience" Sir Gallen thought as he was beginning to read the timing of Banneck's blade.

"Fight me you coward!" Banneck yelled as Gallen was avoiding every strike yet not returning the strikes. "Patience" Gallen thought again as he ducked under a head strike. Banneck was fed up and increased the speed and intensity of his strikes as he began to

become more careless in the assault. Soon Banneck was slowing down and threw everything he could into a waist level cut at the boy when Gallen took the opportunity to capitalize on the angry knight's impatience. Gallen jumped just out of range of the wild strike and while Ser Banneck was recovering from the swing Gallen dashed forward and brought his sword up across the chest and chin of the angry warrior.

The whole crowd fell silent and Sir Gallen knelt by the knight feeling like the whole ordeal was a shame. Lord Banneck felt as though he must protect his pride and by doing so left Sir Gallen no choice. "He basically defeated himself," Gallen thought as he remembered what his father said. "A man who controls his spirit can rule kingdoms, but a man who cannot, shall not live long."

Every great warrior is tested and tempted. Some persevere through the trials and are able to deny the temptations. Unfortunately, there are many others who buckle under the weight of their hardships or succumb to the pleasures of temptation. Those who do are known as the Counterfeit Warrior or the Tainted Champion. Here are some of the traits associated with these Tainted Champions.

THE COUNTERFEIT WARRIOR MINDSET

⊕ **Bloodthirsty Barbarian (Violent)** - The tainted warrior has an insatiable bloodlust and never shies away from violence even when a more peaceful option is present.

The LORD trieth the righteous: but the wicked and him that loveth violence his soul hateth. - Psalm 11:5

Then said Jesus unto him, Put up again thy sword into his place: for all they that take the sword shall perish with the sword. - Matthew 26:52

⊕ **Selfish and not a Team Player** - He is selfish and out for his own gain. He doesn't work well with others but instead uses them to get ahead.

Two are better than one; because they have a good reward for their labour. - Ecclesiastes 4:9

Bear ye one another's burdens, and so fulfill the law of Christ. - Galatians 6:2

⊕ **Double-minded** - He is swayed by every passing opinion and not confident. He has no steady ground to stand on and his mind is torn.

But let him ask in faith, nothing wavering. For he that wavereth is like a wave of the sea driven with the wind and tossed...A double minded man is unstable in all his ways. - James 1:6-8

No man can serve two masters: for either he will hate the one, and love the other; or else he will hold to the one, and despise the other. Ye cannot serve God and mammon. - Matthew 6:24

⊕ **Angry Bully** - He is an overpowering, domineering bully who preys on the weak and takes the easy road over the honorable road.

Thou shalt not avenge, nor bear any grudge against the children of thy people, but thou shalt love thy neighbor as thyself: I am the LORD. - Leviticus 19:18

For God hath not given us the spirit of fear; but of power, and of love, and of a sound mind. - 2 Timothy 1:7

⊕ **Impatient / Impulsive** - His anger leads to his impatience and impulsiveness. He acts instantly, driven by the flesh and not the spirit.

He that hath no rule over his own spirit is like a city that is broken down, and without walls. - Proverbs 25:28

He that is slow to wrath is of great understanding: but he that is hasty of spirit exalteth folly. - Proverbs 14:29

The Tainted Champion has more in common with the Nephilim than he does with his fellow man. He is a bloodthirsty, rage-filled, loose cannon who loses his cool at the slightest sign of things not going his way. Even boredom alone can lead this trouble maker to bully others for the "fun" of it. They live and die by the sword and are masters of revenge. They take "an eye for an eye" to a whole other extreme and demand more than equal payback for any wrong done to them. The Lord will require their blood soon enough for the innocent blood they have shed (Genesis 9:5-6) and we know that our King never draws His sword in vain (Romans 13:4). These oppressors of men are hated by our King and their reign of terror finds no limits (Psalm 11:5).

THERE'S N⊕ "I" IN TEAℳ

Our Lord tells us that two are better than one and that they will receive a good reward for their joint labor (Ecclesiastes 4:9). We also know that iron sharpens iron and a man sharpens his friend (Proverbs 27:17). We are all members of one body (1 Corinthians 12:20-25) however these dark warriors are an army of one. They are lovers of themselves, covetous, boasters, proud, blasphemers, disobedient to their parents, unthankful, and unholy men of the flesh (2 Timothy 3:2-4). Were they to see a brother in need they would scoff and continue walking right past them, cheerfully thinking "Better him than me!" (1 John 3:17). They do not care how pleasant it may be to dwell together in unity and join forces as a team (Psalm 133:1) because it would not only take the spotlight off of them but they might even for once not get their way! Oh, the thought alone might kill them! It is not good that man should be alone (Genesis 2:18) but these men are destined to live a life of loneliness save for the misled women and weak bottom feeding men that surround them unable to break free from their manipulations. They are vain and jealous men provoking others to wrath (Galatians 5:26), which they will gladly partake in as well. Strife follows them like a lost dog and their lives are filled with confusion and pain caused by living after one's own way and ignoring the King's commands (James 3:16). They choose to make earthly treasure their god as they live for the here and now ignoring the hereafter (1 Timothy 6:17-19). Let none of us ever give in to pride and rage lest we slowly morph into these Tainted Champions of self-destruction.

These imitation heroes have no rule over their spirit and are like a city with broken down walls (Proverbs 25:28). Some you will find giving in to drunkenness and soon after wrath, forsaking the sound mind that The Lord offers for a clouded inebriated existence (2 Timothy 1:7). The only thing they hold onto longer than their pride is a grudge as they spew obscenities and vulgarities, disrespecting women and men alike (Ephesians 4:29). They treat women like objects and men like pawns. Those who can deal with this Dark Warrior offer nothing but a leech on his resources and horrible counsel as he sits in his throne of scorn shrouded in darkness (Psalm 1:1). He is always looking over his shoulder and always looking for an advantageous scenario to profit himself. These men have an ever-expanding, never-filled, God-sized hole in their chest that they try to fill with drugs, alcohol, and sex. They hate their fellow man but the saddest part of all is that behind all that pride and bravado some of them actually hate themselves more. These empty heroes have lost sight of their Father if they ever even had it to begin with.

TW⊕ ᙏINDS ARE BE++ER +HAN ⊕NE? I THINK N⊕+!

One of the worst things that plague the Counterfeit Warrior is the curse of double-mindedness. I believe many of us have suffered from this as well or are still suffering from it as I myself struggled with this. It can come from demonic oppression or just a lack of knowledge, faith, or understanding of God's word and will. Even a lack of commitment to God's Word can induce this. The double-mind is torn, two opposing directions and paralyzed by indecision on which direction to go. It is a life filled with compromises and uncertainty. The double-mind is torn, deciphering between Yahweh's will and the will of its own lusts. If you have an unsurrendered heart or unaddressed sin, your spiritual vision begins to be clouded. It is a never-ending, personalized and confusing cloud that rests over your decision making. This will utterly rob you of your peace and leave you feeling uneasy and unsettled. You are left like a wave in the ocean that is tossed back and forth at every gust of wind.

> But let him ask in faith, nothing wavering. For he that wavereth is like a wave of the sea driven with the wind and tossed. - James 1:6

> A double minded man is unstable in all of his ways - James 1:8

A biblical example of double-mindedness is King Saul. One minute he loved David and the next he was throwing a spear at him. One minute he is offering David his daughter and the next he is leading an all-out manhunt to kill David. No matter how many times David proved his loyalty to him, Saul's double-mind would turn him against his friend. King Saul was a man plagued by a double-mind. He claimed to serve God but instead of choosing God's will he made his own unlawful sacrifice before war and ignored the Father. When God's prophet left him and prophesied doom over him, he was heartbroken and regretted the path his double-mind led him down. Saul then sought out a medium (psychic) to contact Samuel for advice. He was a divided man and served two mental masters. You could tell from reading about Saul that the man had no peace. This is the sad fate of the double-minded.

You cannot live a successful life of faith if you cannot make adequate choices. How do you fix this? Our King tells us to draw close to Him, cleanse our hands of sin, and purify our hearts through prayer (James 4:8). We are to submit ourselves to God and resist the devil causing him to flee from us (James 4:7). You must also know the Word of God well and study it to see what it says about any activities or thoughts you may be involved in. If you are unsure if something is okay for you to do or if it is a sin then you need to research God's word for find the answers while seeking Him in prayer. He gives the answer to us freely and does not hide them from His faithful children. The enemy blinds the eyes of unbelievers against God and if possible, he would blind believers from the Word of God too (2 Corinthians 4:4)! I can't stress this fact enough: You need to pray, pray, and PRAY more as you search out the direction you need to go. We are called to be doers of the word and not just hearers only or else we will be deceived (James 1:22). We are not alone in this and nothing is afflicting us that hasn't already afflicted other believers or that our God hasn't been through. Walk in the Spirit and you will start to refrain from fulfilling the lusts of the flesh (Galatians 5:16).

In closing, if you want to live a life of peace and true heroism you must flee from the double-minded, impulsive, angry and self-serving life of the Tainted Champion. These behaviors will try to creep into our lives any chance they get and we must never be comfortable drifting towards these destructive patterns.

CHAP+ER 17

THE PRIES+

The wind had been slamming the trees against the side of the church building all night long as the priest thanked his Father always for His loving protection. "I'm cold," said the young girl who sat in her mother's arms playing with a loose white strand from her dress between her fingers. Her mother stared off into the distance as she had for the last three hours, lost in the deep recesses of another world. Trying to escape from her current life hoping that if she focused hard enough, she could remain in her daydreams until The Lord reclaimed her soul. She never told the priest what exactly happened but he remembered all too well how he found her.

She was the miller's daughter. She and the girl had been there since the priest shut the huge church doors earlier that evening. He found them by the altar after he dealt with the raiders and immediately put his robes over her and the girl. The priest went to fetch the only loaf of bread left in the whole church...and maybe even the whole town. He was starving but he knew he had to save it in case someone else had a greater need. He was used to living off of little but scriptures and prayer. "The Lord is my shepherd," he told himself smiling "I shall not want." He lived in the small town on the outskirts of the Castle Karsmire's boundaries. They never had many visitors...or protection. Being so close to the King's Road meant many the shady fellow would pass by and miss the hidden path that led to the town.

Soon after the castle was taken, the small town was discovered and set upon. The priest was gathering firewood when he saw the raiding party charge into the town and start burning buildings and taking women. They had the miller by the throat as they ran him through with the blade. The whole town seemed lost and all the priest could do was call out to his Father above and pray for mercy. While he was broken and deep in prayer, he knew he had to hide but something wouldn't let his feet move. After about thirty seconds the miller's daughter came out of the stable running full speed and with a torn dress and bloody lip. "Let me go!" she yelled and soon the priest saw the reason why she blazed towards him. He caught her in his arms and without thinking yelled "Quickly! Into the church!" The church was the only building in town made of stone and sealed from the inside with a heavy wooden plank that nearly took two men to lift. The priest had grown accustomed to lifting it on his own and it laid on the inside of the building when he came to collect wood. She ran inside and he heard the old creaky door slam shut as she fastened the minor lock but not the wooden plank. The two raiders came up to the priest and grabbed him by the hair yanking him to the ground. "Why'd ya ledder go ya old fool!? We was havin' fun!" The bigger man in the black steel great helm was obviously the leader and he tightened his grip around the priest's neck. The other man was silent but no less terrifying in his studded leather chest plate and black and red helm with the Hammer Fist crest of the South Lake Raiding Band.

"Father, please let your will be done and if these men can be spared please blind them and cast them away. Thank you always for your loving protection." prayed the priest aloud. "Yer God can't save you, holy man." The one in the black steel armor said as he pulled the priest up to his face and held his hand up with a small dagger threatening to end the priest on the spot. The priest continued in prayer "Father, please spare the souls of these men and let them escape with their lives. Please don't hurt them too badly. Give them a chance to repent and Father, thank you always for your loving protection." The smaller raider went back to the stables where the priest could hear the crying of a young girl. The man in the black steel ran the blade across the priest's cheek slicing it almost to the bone. The priest just stared at him unblinking and unaffected. "Repent while you still draw breath. You don't have to do this; my Father will forgive if you but drop the weapon and leave the woman and the girl behind." "Yer crazy! Brave I'll give you that...but crazy. Why wud I leave. Yer God is absent priest, just as he 'as been absent m'whole life as well."

The priest looked into the bandit's eyes and started to tear up. "You cannot kill me. I am already dead. And I cannot stand by idly while you intend harm upon these women. I don't have a blade or staff but I do not wish to kill you, only to spare you."

The raider in the black armor was shocked. How could a man on the verge of death be so calm? He wasn't used to people not fearing him and it reminded him of a better time that he would rather forget. It reminded him of when he was a child before he became corrupted. He used to play with the other young village boys by the creek using sticks as swords. This was until that tragic day where his family was killed by a similar group of raiders who then kidnapped him and taught him their ways.

The big man snapped back out of his cruel daydream and addressed the priest. "Spare me?! If yer God was real then my life wudda bin dif'rent. I wudn't have been robbed of my youth and along with it my fam'ly." The raider was getting angry and wondering why he didn't just end the man right there.

"I'm sorry," said the priest, "I'm sorry for what evil men have done to you. It wasn't your fault that they set you on this wretched path. My God is real and He will prove to you. Leave this day, you, your friend and the rest of you. Leave this town behind and also this lifestyle of pain. It is never too late. If you do this, He will show you the way. I have some silver pieces in the back of the church hidden under a rock. Let us go gather them and you can use them to buy your way out of this life."

The raider was stunned. He had never once in his life been treated like this. He had held anger against this God, whoever He was, for robbing him of his family and his life. But now for the first time ever, that God felt like He had reached out to him...a dirty murdering criminal. Just then the man's partner came around the corner with a weeping young girl over his shoulder. "Let's go, boss, kill tha fool and let's be off!"

The man in the black armor stood there, angry at the priest for what he had done. It was almost as if the priest killed him. The old him at least. The man loosened his grip on the priest and whispered a very small "thank you" as he walked to his partner. "Leave the girl," he told him. "But boss we aren't to leave any survivors!" said the man in the red and black helmet.

"DO AS I SAY! Our business here is done. Grab the horses and let the others know. And leave the girl, we don't have any room fer extra mouths." commanded *the large man in the black armor. The smaller bandit did as he was told and the small girl ran to the priest as he picked her up and prayed to his Father "Thank you always for providing your loving protection." He ran back to the church as the sunset and the rain started pouring. He lifted the heavy wooden plank into its slots behind the church doors and ran to the woman with the young girl by his side. As soon as the woman saw the girl, they both cried out and the girl ran to the woman's arms and they remained there for the next three hours.*

He couldn't forget how it all happened and now as he stood staring at the woman and the girl later into the night, he handed them the last piece of bread in the whole village and he prayed with them. "Thank you, Father, for providing a way out for that man and for all of us here. Thank you always for your loving protection."

We must now learn about the holy and devout side of the Warrior-Priest... The Priest. The mindset of The Priest embodies many things. Dedication and discipline to studying and living the Word of God. Longsuffering and patience when dealing with trials and tribulations. Selfless in service and ruler over his spirit. The Priest draws his purpose from fulfilling Yahweh's will on Earth over his own. He keeps his flesh under subjection by fasting and replacing physical bread with spiritual bread from the Word of God. He flees from unrighteousness and filth to maintain holiness before Father God because He is holy (1 Peter 1:16). The priest is always quick to forgive those who wrong him as he knows his Father is quick to forgive him of his trespasses. The spotlight is always on The Priest's behavior and he stands as an example of how one should live when he is seeking after God. Any careless or lax approach to his behavior can have repercussions extending to those who look to him as an example or as an indictment for those who wish to see him fall. Now we will examine some of the traits that are associated with The Priest Mindset.

THE PRIEST MINDSET

⊕ **Holy, Pure and Consecrated** - Since our God is holy, The Priest knows that he is also to be holy. The Priest knows that without holiness he will never be able to see The Lord or enter into the holiest of holies.

Because it is written, Be ye holy; for I am holy. - 1 Peter 1:16

Follow peace with all men, and holiness, without which no man shall see the Lord - Hebrews 12:14

⊕ **Forgiveness** - A priest is very aware of how much his Father in heaven has forgiven him his trespasses, therefore, he should be quick to forgive others, seeing the importance of the cleansing of sin and possible reconciliation.

If we confess our sins, he is faithful and just to forgive us our sins, and to cleanse us from all unrighteousness. - 1 John 1:9

⊕ **Disciplined** - The priest must exhibit a life devoted to discipline. It takes discipline to keep learning scriptures and correcting oneself. He mustn't give up or grow lazy. It also takes a submitted man to accept discipline from The Lord.

Whoso loveth instruction loveth knowledge: but he that hateth reproof is brutish. - Proverbs 12:1

But I keep under my body, and bring it into subjection: lest that by any means, when I have preached to others, I myself should be a castaway. - 1 Corinthians 9:27

Now no chastening for the present seemeth to be joyous, but grievous: nevertheless afterward it yieldeth the peaceable fruit of righteousness unto them which are exercised thereby. - Hebrews 12:11

⊕ **Selfless Servant** - The Priest knows that he is called to esteem others higher than himself and he understands the importance of sacrifice. Combining the two concepts should be natural to him as it is to his God.

Let nothing be done through strife or vainglory; but in lowliness of mind let each esteem others better than themselves. - Philippians 2:3

Greater love hath no man than this, that a man lay down his life for his friends. - John 15:13

⊕ **Longsuffering** - The Priest must be longsuffering since he has seen, up close, Yahweh's longsuffering for himself. Along with being in close proximity to the Father comes a closer examination of our own hearts.

Put on therefore, as the elect of God, holy and beloved, bowels of mercies, kindness, humbleness of mind, meekness, longsuffering - Colossians 3:12

We are called to be priests who are a chosen generation, a royal priesthood, a holy nation, and a peculiar people to praise the God who has called us out of the darkness and into His marvelous light (1 Peter 2:9). We are made kings and priests unto Yeshua and His Father (Revelation 1:6) to offer up our spiritual sacrifices to be accepted before our God (1 Peter 2:5). As we are a kingdom of priests and a holy nation (Exodus 19:6) made to reign on Earth in the coming age, we must lay aside all malice, guile, hypocrisies, envies and all evil speakings (1 Peter 2:1-3) so we can know that our Lord is good. For when we were rejected by humans we were also accepted by God (1 Peter 2:4). He has chosen us for this role and ordained us so that we can now bring forth fruit in our Father's name that will remain and receive anything that we ask in His name that is according to His will (John 15:16).

Now, let's get some back story into biblical priests. The Hebrew word for priest is *"kohen"* or *"kahan"* and can be applied to "one who ministers." It can also describe an individual who was set apart for duties relating to worship and ministering as a priest. The Greek word used for priest is *"hiereus"* and it means "a priest, one who offers sacrifice to a god." In ancient times, before the office of priest was introduced, every man performed priestly duties for himself offering sacrifices for his own sin. Soon after, the head of the household would offer sacrifices for his family. Eventually, the role would be assigned to the tribe of Levi and them alone. The qualifications to become a Levite priest were very specific. Since Yahweh is holy and Yeshua was the "spotless lamb without blemish," He expects His priests to be without blemish. This was to show how holy He was and to point to the future spotless lamb that would come to save His people. To be a Levite priest you couldn't be female, blind, lame, have a mutilated face, a limb too long, an injured foot or hand (foreshadowing to the nails in Yeshua's feet and hands?), have a hunchback, be a dwarf, have a defect in your sight, have an itching disease, scabs, or crushed testicles (Leviticus 21:16-23).

When it came to the duties of the priest, they were not only in charge of making sacrifices before God for themselves and for the people but also discern God's will for the people. This task was eventually taken over by the scribes. The priests were also in charge of accepting tithes and offerings. God had his people give a tithe to the Levite priests since their job was solely to tend to the matters of Yahweh, therefore, they had little time left to provide food for themselves among other things. They would be in charge of blessing people and sometimes even assist in legal matters. It was also up to the priests to take care of the temple. Now that we have become priests through Yeshua it is up to us to care for the temple. However, the temple we care for is the Temple of the Holy Spirit which rests inside of every believer.

What? know ye not that your body is the temple of the Holy Ghost which is in you, which ye have of God, and ye are not your own?
For ye are bought with a price: therefore glorify God in your body, and in your spirit, which are God's.
- 1 Corinthians 6:19-20

CHAPTER 18
THE HOLY PRIEST AND THE LIVING TEMPLE

*Follow peace with all men, and holiness, without which
no man shall see the Lord - Hebrews 12:14*

Since our bodies are temples of the Holy Spirit, we must treat it as such. You would not bring drugs into God's temple. Nor would you fornicate within its gates. You would not put up posters of satanic imagery or give offerings to demons. Sadly enough, this is how many people are treating their temples. They are profaning what is supposed to be holy. Our God has called us to holiness but we are filling our temples with uncleanness and evil decorations. Like a black sludge smeared on a white garment, we are defiling the very house of the Holy Spirit!

For God hath not called us unto uncleanness, but unto
holiness. - 1 Thessalonians 4:7

We all have a past that comes with a history of many sins. The problem comes when we carry those same sins into our new life and fail to confront them and remove them from our temples. Picture a man buying a building he wishes to convert to a church, but upon inspection, it has pornographic posters on the walls. He would *never* leave those posters up and open the doors to his church without tearing them down first. We must also tear down these things from our walls. We are told that our war is not against flesh and our weapons are not carnal or of this world. Our weapons of warfare are mighty through God and are used for the pulling down of strongholds. What is a stronghold? A stronghold is a castle! A fortified castle of sin that has set up it's a fortress on your land! We are given spiritual catapults to destroy that castle and root out all the sin that remains so deeply planted in our deceitful hearts.

> For though we walk in the flesh, we do not war after the flesh: **(For the weapons of our warfare are not carnal, but mighty through God to the pulling down of strongholds;)** Casting down imaginations, and every high thing that exalteth itself against the knowledge of God, and bringing into captivity every thought to the obedience of Christ; - 2 Corinthians 10:3-5 (emphasis added)

The sins of our former life do not usually disappear when we start to follow Yeshua or even if we have been following him for decades. They have to be dealt with individually, by us personally. Just like the care of the temple was up to the priest, the care of our personal temples is up to us as the new priests. We are to cleanse ourselves from all filthiness of the flesh *and* spirit, perfecting holiness in the fear of God (2 Corinthians 7:1). We must destroy the former lusts of our flesh that we took up in our ignorance and turn the other way from them as one would turn from a deadly viper (1 Peter 1:14-16).

Without holiness, we can never see the face of our holy Lord (Hebrews 12:14). He is a holy God and will not tolerate sin in His direct presence. This is why the priests had to maintain a very high degree of holiness before entering the deepest part of the tabernacle, the holy of holies. The priests had to make many offerings and had to strictly adhere to all the proper protocols and procedures and even then, they could only enter into the holy of holies once a year on the Day of Atonement. In our day and age, the veil has been torn and we are able to have His Holy Spirit dwell within us. We know that Yahweh does not change (Malachi 3:6) and this should trigger the fear of The Lord in us all into taking better care of our temples.

Sin is a destructive all-consuming disease but the holiness of Yahweh is an all-consuming fire that leaves nothing behind. We are now kings and priests unto God and must make offerings of peace and thanksgivings for everything He does for us and even thanks just for who He is. We simply cannot leave sin in our temples. If you have a pornography addiction you are not only destroying your view of women and destroying the relationship with your spouse but also allowing demons into the same place that even *priests* had to be clean to enter! Sin tends to cloak us in shame and cause us to recoil from the light of God. I will tell you something a pastor once told me that changed my life. Somehow the topic of masturbation came up and he said this: "People will tell you that everyone does it and that is simply not true. I don't do it. I'm telling you right now that I don't do that so there is at least one person that doesn't do it. Don't let people's lies and their own sin make you feel like it's okay to participate." That changed how I viewed things. That sin was something I just assumed everyone did but once he said that to me, I completely stopped participating in that sin! Praise be to God alone, for it was His truth spoken through that pastor that was able to shine His marvelous light on a dark sin that was in my life at the time.

> But ye are a chosen generation, a royal priesthood, an holy nation, a peculiar people; that ye should shew forth the praises of him who hath called you out of darkness into his marvelous light - 1 Peter 2:9

Do not let anyone else's uncleanness make you comfortable with your sin. If we purge ourselves of these sins, we shall become a vessel of honor that is sanctified (declared holy) and prepared for the Master to use us for the good work we have been assigned (2 Timothy 2:21). Just as the weapons of our warfare are spiritual our armor is as well. Now you can equip your next piece of armor that is vital to our holiness... The Breastplate of Righteousness.

THE BREASTPLATE OF RIGHTEOUSNESS

Stand therefore, having your loins girt about with
truth, and having on the breastplate of righteousness -
Ephesians 6:14

The Greek word used for breastplate is "*thorax*" and the Greek word used for righteousness is "*dikaiosune*" which can mean righteousness or justice. The purpose of a breastplate is to protect your vital organs from attack. Your heart needs protection as does your body which is the temple of the Holy Spirit. Our Father gives us a clean and fresh breastplate with His righteousness on it and He expects us to maintain the care of this breastplate by living a righteous life every single day. We know that our righteousness is as filthy rags to Him, however, we are to still walk out our lives the way He asks us to. Think of it like this, His righteousness made the breastplate effective and our righteous living is the polishing of the grime of sin from the surface of the breastplate. The putting on and the care of this armor lies on the individual. When we fail to put the breastplate on and choose to not live righteously, we are swinging the castle door wide open for the demonic forces of the dark lord to rush in and assault us. When we catch the traitor who has opened the gates to the enemy and we uncover his identity we find out that he is actually our "old man" or old self! The person who we were before Christ serves a different master. Our old self is in service to Lord Lucifer and all of his dark minions. When we let the old man rear his ugly head, we bring the counsel of the dark one into our camp to whisper foul guidance into our ears. The old man is corrupted by his deceitful lusts. We must renew our minds and walk in the ways of the new man who is created in righteousness and true holiness.

> That ye put off concerning the former conversation the
> **old man**, which is corrupt according to the deceitful
> lusts; and be renewed in the spirit of your mind; and
> that ye put on the new man, which after God is created
> in righteousness and true holiness. - Ephesians 4:22-24
> (emphasis added)

The old man can be starved and subdued by us living as the new man, however, he is never fully defeated until we enter into the heavenly kingdom. The old man will always rise from the dead given the chance and if we live unrighteously we raise him up and reinstate him in our war council. The old man is driven by sinful cravings and will always try to lead you toward unrighteousness. When we leave the old man alone for too long his sinful cravings grow even worse and branch out into more deadly sins and worse habits than what he started with. With Satan's forces working in tandem with the old man, we will be turned from the path of righteousness and left on the road of impurity, lovelessness, and bondage to sin as our new master. The old man wants us to lie, steal, grow bitter, act in anger, be vulgar, curse, tear down others, tell filthy jokes, and lose all respect for our fellow man. The new man, however, is a righteous knight who walks a path of truth, deals with his anger, builds up his brothers, forgives others, and has purity in speech with a grateful heart. This new man is born when we come into a relationship with Yeshua and we must help him to grow stronger every day. If we practice righteous living, confess our sins to our Father, and become accountable to another brother in Christ, we can ensure that we leave no room for the resurrection of the old man. The old man is at war with our King and the new man is allied with the King to destroy the enemy. We must serve God and not sin.

> Neither yield ye your members as instruments of
> unrighteousness unto sin: but yield yourselves unto
> God, as those that are alive from the dead, and your
> members as instruments of righteousness unto God.
> - Romans 6:13

We are to live by the standard the Word of God sets for us and not by worldly standards. We mentioned earlier that asking someone if they think they are going to heaven often gets you the answer "I think I am, I'm a good person." Being a good person is not a substitute for obeying God and living how he tells us too. Living unrighteously leaves us open to demonic oppression and gives the enemy a foothold onto our castle wall to climb into our lives and wreak havoc. Any activity related to the occult, sorcery, or magic is detestable to The Lord and is another example of unrighteousness.

> There shall not be found among you any one that maketh his son or his daughter to pass through the fire **(idolatry)**, or that useth divination **(fortune telling/ tarot)**, or an observer of times **(omens)**, or an enchanter, or a witch. Or a charmer, or a consulter with familiar spirits **(psychic / medium)**, or a wizard **(witchcraft/ occult)**, or a necromancer **(consults dead)**. For all that do these things are an abomination unto the Lord: and because of these abominations, the Lord thy God doth drive them out from before thee. - Deuteronomy 18:10-12 (commentary added).

Now let us examine chapter five of Galatians for other works of the flesh that are at war with those Warrior-Priests wishing to walk righteously.

> Now the works of the flesh are manifest, which are these; Adultery, fornication, uncleanness, lasciviousness, idolatry, witchcraft, hatred, variance, emulations, wrath, strife, seditions, heresies, envyings, murders, drunkenness, revellings, and such like: of the which I tell you before, as I have also told you in time past, that they which do such things shall not inherit the kingdom of God. - Galatians 5:19-21

All of these things have no place in the life of a knight in Yahweh's army who is wearing his Breastplate of Righteousness and the punishment for such is banishment from the Kingdom of God. This road only leads to the destruction of our souls and the loss of an eternity with the one who created us by hand and breathed the breath of life into us. What Galatians also tells us is what to replace those things with. The fruits of the spirit are like reinforcements on the Breastplate of Righteousness making it stronger and more fortified against evil.

> But the fruit of the Spirit is love, joy, peace, longsuffering, gentleness, goodness, faith, Meekness, temperance: against such there is no law. - Galatians 5:22-23

I pray that we all can learn to live out each one of these gifts and be quick to return to them if we ever stray. Every worthy priest should research these gifts and find areas in his life that are not yet yielded over to the Father's will. Subdue the old man and replace him with the new. Equip the Breastplate of Righteousness daily and live the way God intended His people to live. If we ever are confused or unsure about how to live, we have a High Priest of the Order of Melchizedek who showed us the perfect example of priestly excellence. He is High Priest Yeshua.

CHAPTER 19
THE COUNTERFEIT PRIEST

You borrowed my horse when you needed a steed
But I couldn't find you when I was in need
You gave me a gift and you said it was free
Then later you came seeking money from me
You said that I really should work on my anger
Then yelled at me fiercely while deep in your tankard
You told me that my views on scripture were wrong
You sounded to me like a loud clanging gong
You told me that "No one can judge me but God"
When I showed you scripture you look at me odd
I said that I wished to fast in proper ways
You told me you've already fasted ten days
The more that I know you the more you show me
That I've never known such a great Pharisee!

Time for us to address what I like to call the Pharisee Affair. There is a rampant infection in many professing believers that is causing them to act not as holy priests unto The Lord but as "*komer*" in the Hebrew tongue or "Idolatrous Priests" in English. They have also been known as The False Priest, The Holy Hypocrite, the stereotypical megachurch televangelist or even the cult leader. I will say there is nothing wrong with a huge church so long as it follows the Word of God. We all have seen far too many times the megachurch that has grown large from feeding off the pockets of its sheep. With every good man there comes a thousand cheap imitators to try and ride the coattails of his success and for the man of God it is no different. They are wolves in sheep's clothing who seek to profit from the pain of others. They are self-righteous "know it all's" who are quick to point out the speck in a brother's eye but slow to pull the ark sized plank from their own. Let's see some of these disgusting traits of the Counterfeit Priest aka the modern-day Pharisee.

THE COUNTERFEIT PRIEST MINDSET

⊕ **Loveless** - The Counterfeit Priest may profess all day long that they are loving but their actions betray them and show otherwise. You will soon know them by their fruit.

> Though I speak with the tongues of men and of angels, and have not charity, I am become as sounding brass, or a tinkling cymbal. - 1 Corinthians 13:1

> He that saith he is in the light, and hateth his brother, is in darkness even until now. - 1 John 2:9

⊕ **Self-Serving and Twist Scripture** - They twist scripture to serve whatever need they have at the time and wield the Sword of the Spirit in a perverted way to benefit themselves.

I marvel that ye are so soon removed from him that called you into the grace of Christ unto another gospel - Galatians 1:6

For I testify unto every man that heareth the words of the prophecy of this book, If any man shall add unto these things, God shall add unto him the plagues that are written in this book - Revelation 22:18-19

⊕ **Never Wrong** - The Counterfeit Priest will go to great lengths and do verbal gymnastics to get around being wrong. They will tell you something was wrong when you did it but when confronted they say it was different when they did it.

He that covereth his sins shall not prosper: but whoso confesseth and forsaketh them shall have mercy. - Proverbs 28:13

For all have sinned, and come short of the glory of God - Romans 3:23

⊕ **Hypocritical Liars** - They never practice what they preach and constantly lie to others and to themselves.

But woe unto you, scribes and Pharisees, hypocrites! for ye shut up the kingdom of heaven against men: for ye neither go in yourselves, neither suffer ye them that are entering to go in. - Matthew 23:13

⊕ **Self-Righteous and Selfish** - They embody the "holier than thou" persona and are always looking out for themselves before others.

> Take heed that ye do not your alms before men, to be seen of them: otherwise ye have no reward of your Father which is in heaven. - Matthew 6:1

⊕ **Surrounded by other Pharisees** - They are usually surrounded by other like-minded or weak people who will never call them out because of their own sin or weakness. They want to feel safe in their sin so they will not be friends with a righteous person who convicts them.

Be not deceived: evil communications corrupt good manners. - 1 Corinthians 15:33

CHAPTER 20
THE ORDER OF THE
TINKLING CYMBAL

Though I speak with the tongues of men and of angels, and have not charity (**love**), *I am become as sounding brass, or a tinkling cymbal. And though I have the gift of prophecy, and understand all mysteries, and all knowledge; and though I have all faith, so that I could remove mountains, and have not charity* (**love**), *I am nothing. And though I bestow all my goods to feed the poor, and though I give my body to be burned, and have not charity* (**love**), *it profiteth me nothing.*
- 1 Corinthians 13:1-3 (emphasis added)

There is a not so secret society that got its start all the way back at the time of Cain. It is called the Order of the Tinkling Cymbal. The members of this order are characterized by their lack of love. Corinthians makes it clear that if we do all things and have not love, then we are like a sounding brass or a tinkling cymbal and that is precisely what these Counterfeit Priests have become. You know the type. They say they know the Bible well and are quick to shoot off verses to those who are walking in error. They are quick to defend their actions or speak to others about God but something is... missing. They lack the main ingredient to the equation and that ingredient is love. If you do not have love then you do not know the God you profess to know (1 John 4:8). Jesus was asked which is the greatest commandment of all and He gave the two-fold answer of *love* The Lord thy God with all of our heart, soul, mind, and strength and to *love* our neighbor as ourselves (Mark 12:29-31). We are told to put on love, which is the bond of perfectness (Colossians 3:14) and that there is no greater love than to lay down our lives for our friends (John 15:13). The False Priest lacks love and it shows. They are like a clanging cymbal that serves no purpose other than to make noise.

Love requires action. We are told that love covers a multitude of sins (1 Peter 4:8) and that if we love God, we will keep His commandments (John 14:15). Yahweh so loved the world that He took action and gave up His only begotten Son to provide all who believe in Him everlasting life (John 3:16). He took action and loved us first to open the door for us to choose to love Him (1 John 4:19). Yeshua gave us a new commandment that we should love one another as He loved us (John 13:34-35) and that in this love all fear will be cast out (1 John 4:18). A true priest has a relationship with the Father and *knows* Him. If you do not have love then you are by default either an unbeliever, an enemy of God or the dreaded Counterfeit Priest from the Order of the Tinkling Cymbal.

HYPOCRITES, LIARS AND MASTER WORD BENDERS

The Order of the Tinkling Cymbal is also marked by their hypocritical, lying, benders of scripture. These people will have a form of godliness but deny the power thereof (2 Timothy 3:5). They are equipped with their sheep's clothing as they shout of their love of God while denying Him with their actions (Titus 1:16). If you say that you know God but you do not keep His commandments, the Bible makes it very clear that you are a liar and that the truth is not in you (1 John 2:4). They act like they are men of the light but their hate for their brethren shows the darkness of their souls (1 John 2:9). They hold people to a standard that they themselves do not meet (Romans 2:3) all the while ignoring the fact that everything hidden will be revealed and their dark deeds will one day be exposed by the light (Luke 12:2). They are quick to do their deeds while people are watching unknowingly forfeiting their heavenly rewards for earthly trash (Matthew 6:1). They say they are cheerful givers but there always comes a day when they come back asking to be repaid for the great kindness they bestowed upon you. Love doesn't keep score (1 Corinthians 13:4-7) but these priests are better at scorekeeping than any ten tax collectors combined!

These Counterfeit Priests practically make an art form out of twisting scriptures to serve their needs. Their interpretation of scripture is blinded by their own lusts and insatiably itchy ears (2 Timothy 4:3-4). They walk arm in arm with seducing spirits and devour the doctrines of devils practically growing horns of their own above their glowing red eyes (1 Timothy 4:1). They are masters of dividing the flock and make a sport of offending those in the faith (Romans 16:17-20) as they build their phantom kingdoms higher and higher on the heads of those they hurt. Sure, they will tithe when being watched, however, they refuse to do the weightier tasks such as showing mercy (Matthew 23:23). They serve their father the devil with a fervent zeal that would make any true priest jealous were it not used for such evil. They perform great acts of unrighteousness and call it good while hating their brother and calling it love (1 John 3:10). They claim to have a firm grasp on religion yet they have a loose grasp of their own tongue as they carelessly cut others down with their double-edged tongues of venom (James 1:26-27). They are like great white tombs that are polished on the outside to a brilliant shine yet on the inside the spider webs and dust give way to dead men's bones strewn about the catacombs of their souls (Matthew 23:27).

These False Priests should never take us by surprise. Why should they be any different than their father the devil who also is a master of disguise who appears as an angel of light when he is really a serpent of darkness (2 Corinthians 11:14)? One wonders what value they see in proclaiming their faith while having no works to prove it (James 2:14). It should be easy to spot them by their inability to love their brothers which shows that if they can't even master brotherly love then there is no way they can love the Father (1 John 4:20).

Thankfully our King tells us what to do about these foul acolytes when He tells us to withdraw ourselves from every brother that walks disorderly (2 Thessalonians 3:6). These snakes will give you their word then manipulate the situation to sneakily retrieve their word from you and leave you with nothing but empty promises. Their word means nothing and is worthless and when you call them out on it, they are overly offended that you would ever call out such a "holy man or woman of God." We are told to let our NO mean NO and our YES mean YES and that anything else is of the evil one (Matthew 5:37). I guess that shows you who these priests truly serve! If you exhibit any of these traits, it is not too late to lay down your filthy robes of self-righteousness and obtain the robes of Yeshua's righteousness. Repent and turn from this cult of self-servitude.

CHAPTER 21
THE KNIGHT AND THE COUNTERFEIT CRUSADER

Oh, what does it mean Sir to be a good Knight?
To always win tourneys and never lose fights?
To win all the hearts of the fairest of maids?
To have all the bards sing of your accolades?
While they all may seem great and all have their time,
We seem to be missing the point of this rhyme.
Victory is good and yes praise can be more,
But greater reward lies with helping the poor.
While hearts of fair maidens do swell up our pride,
Bard's songs do not fill the great hole that's inside.
Do you know the true secret of every great knight?
It is service to others and being a light.

We are nearing the end of our adventure and for these last couple sections we are going to do something different. We are going to first learn about The Counterfeit Knight before we finish up by learning about the True Knight. We are doing it this way so we can save the best for last and finish our quest with the perfect embodiment of the Lion, Lamb, Warrior, and Priest. He is the Knight! But hold your horses and don't get too excited just yet as we first take a look at this deviant, vile, disgusting, and foul beast...The Counterfeit Crusader!

CHAPTER 22
THE COUNTERFEIT CRUSADER

Lord Karvet was loved by many for his heroic deeds. He had won more tournaments than anyone had ever won. He was a local hero who never had any trouble finding the companionship of women. Yet, no one knew the real him. Lord Karvet had always brought the king more tribute than any of his brothers at arms. Gold was as easy to find for him as water was for a fish. Yet, no one knew the real him. Lord Karvet was a pious man who knew all there was to know about The Lord and he often kept justice in the town full of sinners. Yet, no one knew the real him.

You see Lord Karvet had won more tournaments than anyone else because He had cheated more than anyone else and was one of the most subtle men to ever live. He conned many women into being with him and those who resisted he overpowered by force. He never got caught. Lord Karvet had always brought more tribute than anyone else to the king because he would get drunk and raid the neighboring village with a couple of bandits from the outskirts of town. He would wear his helm not to be detected and would be covered in blood as his pockets were filled with gold. He never got caught.

Lord Karvet was not a pious man as much as he was self-righteous and steeped in false religion. He was paid by the evil Pope Magnesto to remove any who went against the pope's plans to take over the churches in the region. He was a bully who cornered weaker men and pressed upon them until they saw things his way. He never got caught.

But now the day had come where Lord Karvet had fallen from his horse onto a stone bridge during a thunderstorm and as he laid there bleeding out of his head, he felt his life leave him.

He now stood before a glorious man in all white who went over all the evil deeds that Lord Karvet had committed. You see this "man" knew the real Lord Karvet and Lord Karvet was finally caught...

Our last counterfeit is The Counterfeit Crusader. He passes himself off as a hero and uses anything to his advantage to look as good as possible to as many people as possible while having a dark heart and a black soul. The epitome of self-serving, this would-be knight in shining armor is nothing more than a shining serpent in steel. Time to uncover the dark secrets of this plagued villain.

THE COUNTERFEIT CRUSADER MINDSET

⊕ **Preys on the Weak** - The Counterfeit Crusader always takes the low hanging fruit as he picks on those weaker than him. He uses his power for evil instead of for good and is a leech on society. Such great potential wasted on a bully.

Defend the poor and fatherless: do justice to the afflicted and needy. - Psalms 82:3-4

Whosoever hateth his brother is a murderer: and ye know that no murderer hath eternal life abiding in him. - 1 John 3:15

⊕ **Puts on a Mask** - This Counterfeit Knight never shows his true face. He is always faking it and putting on a mask to impress others or to hide his evil personality. You can never get the full picture from this man or trust anything he is putting forth for fear of it being a mask.

Wherefore the Lord said, Forasmuch as this people draw near me with their mouth, and with their lips do honour me, but have removed their heart far from me, and their fear toward me is taught by the precept of men - Isaiah 29:13

Not every one that saith unto me, Lord, Lord, shall enter into the kingdom of heaven; but he that doeth the will of my Father which is in heaven. - Matthew 7:21-23

⊕ **Quits and Complains** - A constant griper and complainer, this man is driven by pride, which leads to protests when things do not go his way. Not only that, but he is the opposite of longsuffering as he gives up on nearly anything he does that gives him the slightest bit of challenge or resistance.

The Lord is not slack concerning his promise, as some men count slackness; but is longsuffering to us-ward, not willing that any should perish, but that all should come to repentance. - 2 Peter 3:9

Do all things without murmurings and disputings
- Philippians 2:14

Let no corrupt communication proceed out of your mouth, but that which is good to the use of edifying, that it may minister grace unto the hearers. - Ephesians 4:29

⊕ **Ruled by Lust and Disrespects Women** - This man has a nearly insatiable sexual appetite and has no respect for women. To him, they are objects of pleasure. His appetite for the other pleasures of the flesh follows suit, as he is driven by the flesh and stifled in spirit.

But I say unto you, That whosoever looketh on a woman to lust after her hath committed adultery with her already in his heart. - Matthew 5:28

This I say then, Walk in the Spirit, and ye shall not fulfil the lust of the flesh. - Galatians 5:16

Rebuke not an elder, but intreat him as a father; and the younger men as brethren; The elder women as mothers; the younger as sisters, with all purity. Honour widows that are widows indeed. - 1 Timothy 5:1-3

⊕ **Respecter of Persons** - Along with wearing a mask, The Counterfeit Crusader seeks to gain favor where he can and will treat people differently based on social rank or on what he stands to gain from them. He is a user and a manipulator who can never be a real friend or ever find real love due to his detachment from human relationships.

For there is no respect of persons with God. - Romans 2:11

There is neither Jew nor Greek, there is neither bond nor free, there is neither male nor female: for ye are all one in Christ Jesus. - Galatians 3:28

⊕ **Puts God Second** - Worst of all, this weak warrior puts himself first and if at all, puts God second. The ruler of the universe takes a backseat to this reckless ogre. Ironic that he ignores the one person who can actually benefit him.

But seek ye first the kingdom of God, and his righteousness; and all these things shall be added unto you. - Matthew 6:33

No man can serve two masters: for either he will hate the one, and love the other; or else he will hold to the one, and despise the other. Ye cannot serve God and mammon. - Matthew 6:24

UNH⊕LY KNIGH✝

This Unholy Knight is a chameleon who passes for a real knight in most circles. Whatever faults of his are discovered, he passes them off as minor yet charming character flaws or funny anecdotes about himself. He covered his misdeeds with the classic line "It was just a joke!"

As a mad man who casteth firebrands, arrows, and death, so is the man that deceiveth his neighbour, and saith, Am not I in sport? **(Only joking)** - Proverbs 26:18-19 (emphasis added)

This spoiled brat is never serious and seems stuck in adolescence. He is also very dangerous and a vicious brute who will bully and manipulate at the drop of a hat. Stealing isn't past him either and he is on a constant quest to acquire as much pleasure as he can for his ravenous flesh that pulls his strings like a puppet. He is like a zombie who is dead inside and seeking entertainment and pleasure to fill that void. He is like an angry bear with a blindfold on drunkenly swiping his way through life leaving a trail of destruction while also harming himself. He is not even safe from his own warpath, as he has a constant chip on his shoulder that he decided he must make the world pay for. He is able to fool most people that he still has some redeeming qualities which keeps them intrigued just long enough to steal, kill, or destroy them one last time. Let us now take a closer look into the life of this Unholy Knight and his band of traveling fools.

CHAP+ER 23
NAYSAYERS AND SERPEN+-+ONGUED WHISPERERS

And Caleb stilled the people before Moses, and said, Let us go up at once, and possess it; for we are well able to overcome it. But the men that went up with him said, We be not able to go up against the people; for they are stronger than we. And they brought up an evil report of the land which they had searched unto the children of Israel, saying, The land, through which we have gone to search it, is a land that eateth up the inhabitants thereof; and all the people that we saw in it are men of great stature. And there we saw the giants, the sons of Anak, which come of the giants: and we were in our own sight as grasshoppers, and so we were in their sight. - Numbers 13:30-33

I n the book of Numbers, you see Caleb returning to his people after being sent to survey and spy out Canaan, the Promised Land. This was the land that God Himself had promised to give to them. His direct will was for the Israelites to conquer this land and dwell in it. Even with the knowledge of the Father's will the Israelites *still* gave a bad report and doubted!

Caleb starts off by calming people down and saying, "Let us go up at once, and possess it for we are well able to overcome it." He was fired up and ready to complete his mission assigned to him from God. What is the first thing that happens after that? He is shot down by the doubting naysayers in the camp. They are poisoning the well as they say, "We be not able to go up against the people; for they are stronger than we." The Bible referred to this report as *evil*. Their open display of doubting God's ability to keep His word and to fulfill His promises was *pure evil*. Their lack of faith in their Deliverer showed when they saw the odds and chose to fear those instead of in Yahweh.

Many times throughout your walk with the Father you will have your thunder stolen by Counterfeit Crusaders who just can't seem to be content. You will have those that see the holy fire burning in you and wish to put it out so their pile of ashes looks less shameful. You will have people who are convicted by your bold display of fearless faith and it will make them uncomfortable. They will sometimes speak out against you and even turn others away from you. Like the Hebrews complaining to Moses about having better food to eat when they were slaves (Exodus 16:3), these people can never be content and will always find something to complain about. One bad apple ruins the whole bunch just as one shield out of formation in a phalanx exposes the rest. "Nay," says the naysayer, "You can't do that. Nay, you won't succeed taking that risk, you will fail! No one does it *that* way, and you are wrong for trying." Insolent do-nothings who seek to bring you down to their level. Like a blacksmith's anvil around your ankle, they seek to never let you get too far away from their own faithless lives.

The Bible has a name for such people and that name is SCOFFER. In fact, Father God thought it such an important matter that He addressed it in the first verse of the first psalm!

Scoffer - someone who jeers or mocks or treats something with contempt or calls out in derision

Blessed is the man that walketh not in the counsel of the ungodly, nor standeth in the way of sinners, nor sitteth in the seat of the scornful (Scoffer in ESV translation). - Psalm 1:1

What does the holy writ say to do with these scoffers? Cast them out!

Cast out the scorner **(Scoffer in ESV)**, and contention shall go out; yea, strife and reproach shall cease - Proverbs 22:10 (Emphasis added)

So, by casting out these naysaying scoffers from your life, you will thereby cast out the contention, strife, and reproach that they create! Hallelujah! Out goes the scoffer and in comes peace.

The next type of person we will get into is the Serpent-tongued Whisperer. These are the type of people who spread lies and cast doubt. These slanderers spread gossip like wildfire through the ranks, weakening the resolve of those around them and keeping them in a pit of low self-confidence and assuredness that The Lord brings.

Just like the doubters in the book of Numbers they brought the false report of imminent defeat to the troops and put the fear of the enemy into the hearts of their kinsmen.

Thou shalt not raise a false report: put not thine hand with the wicked to be an unrighteous witness. - Exodus 23:1

Thou shalt not go up and down as a talebearer **(Slanderer in ESV)** among thy people; neither shalt thou stand against the blood of thy neighbour; I am The Lord. - Leviticus 19:16 (emphasis added)

> Keep thy tongue from evil, and thy lips from speaking guile **(Lies in ESV)** - Psalms 34:13 (Emphasis added)

These Serpent-tongued Whisperers act as bad counselors and bad advisors to your life. They should be purged immediately. If what they do is unintentional, you can try coming to them in love following the protocol listed in Matthew.

> Moreover, if thy brother shall trespass against thee, go and tell him his fault between thee and him alone: if he shall hear thee, thou hast gained thy brother. But if he will not hear thee, then take with thee one or two more, that in the mouth of two or three witnesses every word may be established. And if he shall neglect to hear them, tell it unto the church: but if he neglect to hear the church, let him be unto thee as an heathen man and a publican. - Matthew 18:15-17

If this approach doesn't work then they are a snake in the grass and should be avoided. The effect of bad counsel on your life can be absolutely devastating. It is equivalent to trusting an untrained child with a deadly weapon of war. You set your life in the hands of destruction. Counsel from trusted advisors is crucial to the life of the believer. Our instruction comes from God and our iron is sharpened through wise counsel. You can now see the damaging effects of ineffective battle plans on the war field.

> Without counsel purposes are disappointed: but in the multitude of counsellors, they are established. - Proverbs 15:22

> Be not deceived: evil communications corrupt good manners. - 1 Corinthians 15:33

Last but not least we have one more potential thorn in our side that we need to remove; the grumbler or complainer. We all have a need to share our burdens with others and "vent" out our frustrations to a friend. However, when it goes into the realm of grumbling or complaining we have to take action immediately. It goes without saying that none of you fine knights should let this behavior go unchecked when you find yourself participating in such foul mannerisms.

Do all things without murmurings and disputings - Philippians 2:14

Neither murmur ye, as some of them also murmured, and were destroyed of the destroyer. - 1 Corinthians 10:10

ALWAYS HOPE

Let this be a cautionary tale to anyone who is struggling with these topics we have covered but also remember that there *is* hope. However, change takes COMPLETE surrender. The demons that have latched onto you will *not* give up their champion so easily and you will need to put God first in order to break the control you have let them have over your life. How do I know these counterfeits so well you ask? I speak from experience. I know these counterfeits so well because I have experienced many of these horrible archetypes at numerous times throughout my life. Over the last decade, Father God has been replacing all of my counterfeits with the real versions of these personas and finally, He has brought me to The Warrior-Priest Mindset. My work is not complete nor will it ever be on this side of eternity; however, I am better today than I was yesterday. It is never too late while you are alive and breathing to do as God leads you to do and replace all of these counterfeit behaviors we with the true versions while taking on The Warrior-Priest Mindset as you seek after the King with everything you have. Leave nothing behind and never quit so one day you will hear "Well done, thou good and faithful servant: thou hast been faithful over a few things, I will make thee ruler over many things: enter thou into the joy of thy Lord."

Now that you are familiar with the Counterfeit Crusader, we can address the true Warrior-Priest. The one who rides into battle with a prayer in his heart and a sword in his hand. The one who spends just as much time on his knees in prayer as he does on the field of battle. He is the defender of the weak, the protector of the downtrodden. He is...the Knight!

CHAPTER 24
THE KNIGHT

The knight glared into the eyes of the serpent as it towered over him, pinning him against the wall. This serpent was no ordinary serpent...this was the Nachash. He had six glistening wings and stood like a mane, made of scales and light. His eyes were slits like a snake's eye but they had a hypnotic quality to them. "You dare stare into my eyes, son of Adam?" Nachash said intrigued. "You are a very interesting image. Why does your will not bend like the others?" hissed the serpent. "I'm not like the others." said the knight as he grabbed Nachash's arm and kicked him hard in the chest sending him stumbling back. The Nachash laughed as he slowly slithered back up to the knight. The light from the serpent turned the stone underground passage into a shining hallway. The knight could see rats fleeing from the light and dust falling from the cracks in the stones.

The knight coughed up blood as he regained his footing. His sword was snapped in half under the hoof of the serpent but he still had the Book of the Prophecy tucked away under his breastplate where the serpent couldn't find it. "I have done nothing but provide for you and your kind, knight" the serpent began "I brought truth to your ancestors. Truth and light. Do you know what Yahweh told me about your kind? He said that you are made from the dust to serve Him as dust. He thought it was amusing that you had the key to immortality right next to you but He would never let you have it. I couldn't stand to see Him do to you what He did to me. Did He ever tell you why I was banished from Heaven?"

The Knight gritted his teeth. He knew better than to hold court with this serpent. All the Nachash could do was spew venom and lies, both in equal measure. He was a liar from the start and nothing he said could ever be trusted. The Nachash would say anything to manipulate a situation in his favor, and this time was no different.

"He removed me from His counsel because I defended your father Adam. I told Him that humanity had the divine spark of life and that it was wrong to exclude them and keep them caged in Eden with the common beasts." As the Nachash came closer to the knight his serpentine features began to morph and take on a more sinister look. Horns grew from his head and his mouth filled with fangs. He looked like a dinosaur the knight had seen in the old art scrolls. He looked like...a dragon. The Nachash flashed like a burst of light and all of a sudden, he looked like the most handsome man the knight had ever seen. He flashed back and forth between dragon and man before finally sticking to his human form.

The knight couldn't help but be drawn to the man and he started to take a small step forward. He could feel the angel in his mind and tried with all his might to stop his feet from inching forward.

The angel was covered in armor made of jewels and pipes and the music was making the knight lose control over his will. He fought it and felt like he was losing; however, he kept on fighting.

"All I have ever tried to do was to stop the tyranny of the old man. All I have ever tried to do was to HELP YOU!" Nachash yelled as his angelic face flashed into the face of the dragon on a man's body. After his outburst, his head returned to the handsome hypnotic face covered in a brilliant glow.

"I helped Moses navigate the desert. I helped David slay Goliath. I helped you that night you saved the boy." The knight felt a sharp bolt of pain stab his heart. The memory of the night he saved the boy was burned into his head. The North Tower had been ravaged by the storm and it started to crumble and finally gave way under the pressure. He had searched for hours until he found the boy. His legs were crushed but he was still alive. "You remember. I showed you where the boy was. I kept him alive until you could pry the stones from his limp legs. I breathed life into his dead body. Do you know what I had to give to Yahweh to help you? HE DEMANDED HE KEEP THE WOMAN!" Nachash screamed as he flashed into his full dragon form coiling around the hallway as his leathery wings hovered over the knight.

It pained the knight to hear of his wife. He searched the entire night after rescuing the boy and he couldn't find her body. It wasn't until morning that he found her under the rubble. For a moment he felt angry with God as if it was His fault that she was dead. As he held her one last time, he rebuked the thought and praised his God for their time together. Tears streamed down his face as he recalled that fateful night and he thanked his God again. "Thank you, Father. You gave me time with her before you called her home and you spared the boy." The dragon drew close to the knight and his hot breath burned the skin under the knight's helmet. He had known that his efforts to rehash an old wound in the knight had failed.

"I can feel you call out to him. Tell me the key to the prophecy and I will send you to Him. You will be free poor knight. He is not as you have read in your precious book. He is merciless and genocidal. He wiped out my brothers and left me in this hideous form. What did the old man TELL YOU?"

The knight's will was shaky but he knew His God's will was unshakeable. He had enough of this dragon's lies as he looked above the shining serpents head and saw a stone that looked as if it were about to dislodge. The old catacombs had been on the verge of collapse for years and the knight thought of a lifetime's worth of waiting for his calling finally paying off. He thought of the boy and hoped his grandmother would care for him well. Then he thought of his beautiful wife. Her brown hair, her perfect nose, and her bright eyes. The knight couldn't help but smile. "I will tell you what the key to the prophecy is...though I fear you have already heard of it." said the knight. "Tell me good knight, and I promise I will convince Yahweh to bring the girl back" the dragon lied as his face flashed back to human then to serpent then rested on the dragon form.

The knight removed his helm and began to speak. "It is said that the Great Dragon Slayer will be bruised in the heel by an ancient evil but He will then crush the Dragon's head once and for all. You bruised my heel by taking my bride from me when you shattered that tower. Yet, now I give my life to crush your head. One day the Great Dragon Slayer will fulfill the prophecy but for now, this will have to do!" The knight threw his helmet up toward the loose stone and as the dragon looked up the catacombs started an avalanche of stone covering the dragon and cracking his skull sending light shining everywhere and green blood covering the smashed knight.

Giant chains shot up from under the earth and started to coil around the great dragon's body pulling him through the bottom of the catacombs and into another realm. The knight was passing to the next world and poking out of his breastplate was a small dusty book with the title inscribed on it that read "The Holy Tale of The Great Dragon Slayer Yeshua and the Final Prophecy."

It is TIME! Our entire journey has led up to this point. The KNIGHT. The Knight is the perfect mix of The Warrior and The Priest. Kneeling down on his sword in prayer to his heavenly King. He never runs out of stamina or strength as his source is Father God. He is utterly relentless in battle and maintains his priestly resolve. The patience of The Priest and the ferocity of The Warrior. The power of The Lion bridled by the servant's heart of The Lamb. The defender of the weak. The protector of the downtrodden. He fights not of his own will alone but with the will of the one who sends him. He has the advantage over his opponents due to his one secret weapon...his *faith*. Faith in The Lamb drives the knight to have the bravery of The Lion. He has a priestly heart fixed on honoring God and a warrior's endurance to never leave the battlefield defeated. His life is not his own so he fights like a dead man. He wears his knightly shining armor along with his armor of God. He wields his earthly sword and his sword of the spirit. He is the hero with a lion and a lamb emblazoned on his shield of faith. He rides his white war horse onto the field as many follow behind him. He is the first to charge into battle and the last to leave the church in prayer. He shows no fear, save for the fear of God. Driven by a never-ending fire inside from heaven above, he is set on his mission and unwavering. He is the ultimate knight of Yahweh...THE WARRIOR-PRIEST!

Throughout history, the knight has been the most iconic warrior the world has ever seen. No one can embody what it means to be a true hero more than the knight. The knight is inseparable from his faith. In fact, he is defined by his faith. Fighting with honor and showing mercy to his foes. The knight has The Warrior, The Priest, The Lion, and

The Lamb mindsets all tied into one which makes him the ultimate benchmark for the believer of Yahweh to model himself/herself after aside from Yeshua Himself.

THE C⊕DE ⊕F CHIVALRY

Like I mentioned at the beginning of the book, the knight we are talking about is the romanticized and most readily known version of the knight. We are talking about the knight that comes to mind whenever the topic is brought up as opposed to a fully historically accurate knight. The same goes for the Knight's Code of Chivalry. The real code of chivalry was a code of conduct that started around 1170 A.D. and was a cross between Roman and Germanic practices. It was a code of bravery and basic combat training. Throughout time it evolved into an ever-changing and never consistent basic code of conduct for warriors. What I have done is selected a few traits that embody the spiritual-based side of the knight and a few that embody the physical-based side of the knight. These traits are in no way an exhaustive list but more a guideline for The Warrior-Priest Mindset that I am trying to convey. It is with this mindset that I have approached many situations in my own life and is the framework from which I apply biblical principles to my own life as well. I would describe it as my vehicle to apply God's Word to my own life. It is no replacement for anything in the Word but rather an application tool that has defined a huge part of the calling on my life and my walk with Father.

The Knight of Yahweh lives by a code of chivalry that is based off of the divinely inspired, inherent, and living Word of God. We will highlight several themes now that fit within The Knight Mindset and expand upon them giving a detailed picture of how you will conduct yourself in the service of the King. The traits are divided up by those that come from the priestly nature and those that come from the warrior nature. Let us begin!

THE KNIGHT MINDSET

WARRIOR TRAITS

⊕ **Valor and Courage** - The Knight must be a person of valor who is filled with courage. It is easy to lose heart when you follow your own way and the enemy never stops his war for your soul. You must not lose sight of the King and the courage He bestows upon you. Cowardice is a sin and the Knights in Yahweh's army are anything but cowardly.

> And the angel of The Lord appeared unto him, and said unto him, The Lord is with thee, thou mighty man of valour. - Judges 6:12

> Wait on The Lord: be of good courage, and he shall strengthen thine heart: wait, I say, on The Lord. - Psalms 27:14

⊕ **Perseverance and Resilience** - NEVER SURRENDER! Burn the ships and push forward at all times. You are to run the race in such a way as to win the prize of seeing your Father's face. In all trials and tribulations, it is tempting to give up or to throw in the towel but Jesus never once quit. He is our standard and He stopped at nothing to complete His life's sacrificial mission to save us from bondage to death. You must have the hardiness of a seasoned war veteran and the perseverance of the King.

> If we suffer, we shall also reign with him: if we deny him, he also will deny us; - 2 Timothy 2:12

And let us not be weary in well doing: for in due season we shall reap, if we faint not. - Galatians 6:9

If thou faint in the day of adversity, thy strength is small. - Proverbs 24:10

⊕ **Defender and Protector of the Weak** - Any true knight knows it is his duty to defend the weak and protect those in need. Whether it be a damsel in distress or a burning building of orphans, the knight must always be ready to lay his life down to save others if need be. One of the greatest commandments is to love thy neighbor as thyself and we are to esteem others higher than ourselves. The Knight is given strength by God to fulfill the role of defender and protector.

But if any provide not for his own, and especially for those of his own house, he hath denied the faith, and is worse than an infidel. - 1 Timothy 5:8

And he answering said, Thou shalt love The Lord thy God with all thy heart, and with all thy soul, and with all thy strength, and with all thy mind; and thy neighbour as thyself. - Luke 10:27

⊕ **Heroic Calling** - Every Knight of Yahweh has a divine calling on his life that he or she must never neglect. Their lives are not their own and were bought with a price. The Knight offers his life as a living sacrifice to his King and must never forget his mission. It is to bring glory to the King and always remember that his true Father is awaiting him in eternity.

I therefore, the prisoner of The Lord, beseech you that ye walk worthy of the vocation wherewith ye are called - Ephesians 4:1

Wherefore the rather, brethren, give diligence to make your calling and election sure: for if ye do these things, ye shall never fall - 2 Peter 1:10

Also I heard the voice of The Lord, saying, Whom shall I send, and who will go for us? Then said I, Here am I; send me. - Isaiah 6:8

⊕ **Dragon Slayer** - A staple of every heroic knight is his innate drive to slay dragons. Yeshua is the ultimate dragon slayer and we are made in His glorious image to walk out His will. We are born into this world already enemies of the dragon and will grow strong and be trained in how to make war against the darkness. The quest of the knight is to destroy the dragon's forces until the King calls our life back to Himself. Only then will this phase of the mission be complete.

And I will put enmity between thee and the woman, and between thy seed and her seed; it shall bruise thy head, and thou shalt bruise his heel. - Genesis 3:15

Submit yourselves therefore to God. Resist the devil, and he will flee from you. - James 4:7

And have no fellowship with the unfruitful works of darkness, but rather reprove them. - Ephesians 5:11

PRIEST TRAITS

⊕ **Faith and the Fear of God** - Faith is the primary trait of The Knight. It is the trust and fear of his Father that defines him. Faith is what separates him from all other warriors and the fear of the God of the Bible is what separates him from all other priests. For as many hours as he spends fighting for God, he spends even more sitting at His feet praying and reflecting on His goodness. Prayer is the communication from human to the divine and it goes without saying that this too is a defining trait of this man/woman of God. This is the very heart of The Warrior-Priest.

Now faith is the substance of things hoped for, the evidence of things not seen. - Hebrews 11:1

So then faith cometh by hearing, and hearing by the word of God. - Romans 10:17

Pray without ceasing. - 1 Thessalonians 5:17

Call unto me, and I will answer thee, and shew thee great and mighty things, which thou knowest not. - Jeremiah 33:3

But without faith it is impossible to please him: for he that cometh to God must believe that he is, and that he is a rewarder of them that diligently seek him. - Hebrews 11:6

The fear of The Lord is the beginning of knowledge: but fools despise wisdom and instruction. - Proverbs 1:7

The fear of The Lord is to hate evil: pride, and arrogance, and the evil way, and the froward mouth, do I hate. - Proverbs 8:13

⊕ **Sacrifice and Humility** - We are called to be humble servants of the Most High. If The Knight finds himself in a position of leadership he does well because he is a servant before he is a leader. He leads by example and never becoming puffed up because he knows that his strength and position is not of himself but of his Father in heaven. There is no room for pride when your gifts are from above. He is willing to give it all away and even his own life if that is what his King demands.

I beseech you therefore, brethren, by the mercies of God, that ye present your bodies a living sacrifice, holy, acceptable unto God, which is your reasonable service. - Romans 12:1

For God so loved the world, that he gave his only begotten Son, that whosoever believeth in him should not perish, but have everlasting life. - John 3:16

But he giveth more grace. Wherefore he saith, God resisteth the proud, but giveth grace unto the humble. - James 4:6

For whosoever exalteth himself shall be abased; and he that humbleth himself shall be exalted. - Luke 14:11

⊕ **Justice and Mercy** - The Knight is in love with justice just as his Father is. He obeys the laws of the land but, above that, he obeys the commands of his Father. He does what is right and rights what is wrong. When he does engage in matters of justice, he has a balance of mercy. He is merciful as his Father is merciful and has open ears for those who have fallen on hard times. He uses wisdom to find the perfect balance between justice and mercy because he knows the King values both.

Thus speaketh The Lord of hosts, saying, Execute true judgment, and shew mercy and compassions every man to his brother - Zechariah 7:9

He hath shewed thee, O man, what is good; and what doth The Lord require of thee, but to do justly, and to love mercy, and to walk humbly with thy God? - Micah 6:8

Be ye therefore merciful, as your Father also is merciful. - Luke 6:36

Blessed are the merciful: for they shall obtain mercy. - Matthew 5:7

⊕ **Honor and Purity** - A Knight is a man of honor who honors all around him. He holds himself to a heavenly standard and is constantly maintaining his purity like the kindling of a precious flame on a cold night. He refrains from the lust of the flesh and all other sins that threaten to taint his honor. He knows the importance of being pure so one day he can stand before the King as a clean vessel awaiting use.

Honour all men. Love the brotherhood. Fear God. Honour the king. - 1 Peter 2:17

If a man therefore purge himself from these, he shall be a vessel unto honour, sanctified, and meet for the master's use, and prepared unto every good work. - 2 Timothy 2:21

Blessed are the pure in heart: for they shall see God. - Matthew 5:8

If we confess our sins, he is faithful and just to forgive
us our sins, and to cleanse us from all unrighteousness.
- 1 John 1:9

⊕ **Honesty and Integrity** - Lies are not found in the mouth
of the Warrior-Priest. His "yes" and his "no" are as ironclad as his
armor and he is one of the few men on earth that can be trusted
and taken at his word. He walks in integrity and keeps all perverse
things far removed from his speech.

Lying lips are abomination to The Lord: but they that
deal truly are his delight. - Proverbs 12:22

Providing for honest things, not only in the sight of The
Lord, but also in the sight of men. - 2 Corinthians 8:21

Better is the poor that walketh in his integrity, than he
that is perverse in his lips, and is a fool. - Proverbs 19:1

The integrity of the upright shall guide them: but the
perverseness of transgressors shall destroy them. -
Proverbs 11:3

This is the new Code of Chivalry for The Warrior-Priest. This is
what we live by. The Knight is The Warrior-Priest and this is The
Warrior-Priest Mindset! I pray that this mindset gives you the tools to
now apply these traits directly to your life. All of these traits we have
gleaned from the Holy Word of God and now you must choose to walk
this quest out every single day. Of course, you will fail at times and you
may even find yourself to be the counterfeit version of these heroes
from time to time; however, it is not too late. While there is still breath
in your lungs there is still time to repent and walk in the way of The
Warrior-Priest. We serve a King who is worthy of this task. This side

of eternity is just the beginning and only God knows what awaits us in the next realm. Remember that we must walk in both sides of The Warrior-Priest just as Yeshua walked in both sides of The Lion and The Lamb. You cannot remove the persevering, heroic, and brave strength of the warrior from the patient, longsuffering, merciful heart of the priest. This is the necessary dichotomy for God's chosen Knights and it is up to you to gird your loins with these truths and ready yourself for battle. Wait a tick, what is it that we gird our loins with? That's right, The Belt of Truth!

THE BELT OF TRUTH

Stand therefore, having your loins girt about with
truth… - Ephesians 6:14

ou have now earned your Belt of Truth, but first, you must learn how to wear it and what it means to bear such a vital piece of your knight's regalia.

Jesus saith unto him, I am the way, the truth, and the life:
no man cometh unto the Father, but by me. - John 14:6

Before you equip your Belt of Truth, we must first understand exactly what truth is. Jesus is the truth and so is His word since He is the Word of God. The scriptures were given to us and filled with the Word of God and His divine will. We have all we need between the covers of our Holy Writ. This truth also sets us free from a life of bondage to sin (John 8:32). The greatest ally of The Warrior-Priest is the Holy Spirit of God which is also known as the Spirit of Truth that guides us (John 16:13). When you call upon The Lord in truth, He will be close to you (John 17:17) His loving commandments are far more valuable than any amount of fine gold (Psalm 119:127).

We are called to study the Word to show ourselves approved unto our King as we rightly divide the word of truth (2 Timothy 2:15). Even when we worship The Lord it must be done not only in spirit but also in truth (John 4:24). There are two things The Warrior-Priest always carries, one is his sword and the other is the Word of God. Sometimes they are both one and the same but we will get into that discussion later. We can trust the Word of God because we are told that all scripture is given by inspiration of God and is profitable for doctrine, reproof, correction, and instructions on righteousness (2 Timothy 3:16-17). We are blessed to have the instruction manual to our lives that was directly sent from the Author of Creation.

GIRD THY L⊕INS

It is only by *reading, knowing* and *practicing* the Word of God that we become the best we can be for the Kingdom. His word is a lamp unto our feet and a light unto our path (Psalm 119:105). We live not off of earthly food alone but also the spiritual bread of God's Word (Matthew 4:4). The words of our Lord were written for our learning, that we, through patience and comfort of the scriptures, might have hope. (Romans 15:4). When Jesus was tempted by the devil in the wilderness, He quoted scriptures to Him and then walked out those scriptures with His actions (Matthew 4:1-11). The Word is quick, powerful, and sharper than any two-edged sword piercing asunder the soul and spirit right to the intents of the heart (Hebrews 4:12). The King promises that if we abide in Him, His words shall abide in us and He will grant us whatever we ask according to His will (John 15:7). We need to meditate on His word day and night until it becomes second nature to us (Psalm 1:2). Study and show yourself approved unto God and gird your loins with The Belt of Truth so no man (or entity) can deceive you with lies (2 Timothy 2:15).

EQUIPPING +HE BEL+

The lies of the enemy are designed to lead us off the path of righteousness. Whether it is one degree or one hundred degrees off the path, it makes no difference to the father of lies. He beguiled Eve in the garden into choosing against God's will (John 8:44). Our Father has laid out a set of commands that lead us to a peaceful mind and a path littered with blessings with a way out of any hardship. The enemy is intent on bringing as much pain and strife into the life of the believer as he can and seeks to minimize any blessing upon their lives.

The enemy uses everything from your own family to pop culture to weave his web of lies around us. Just about everything on the television and in music is driven by some sort of satanic agenda or at the very least plays expertly to human lusts of the flesh. Satan is the ruler of this world (1 John 5:19) and he seeks to replace true worth for worthlessness. He lights a fire of dark passion in humans to seek after material possessions or fame among men instead of seeking to please God or to sacrificially provide for his family.

We need the Belt of Truth more than ever to brace the core of our being against wave after wave of constant lies sent from the enemy's camp. Put these words from our Holy Scriptures into practice. Do *not* be like the man who knows the storm is coming but still doesn't prepare as he tells others, "Oh, there's a storm comin' alright." What use does that knowledge do him when he's face down in the waters from not putting his truths to action? We are the children of light and it's about time we step out of the darkness. The light exposes everything for what it is and all of our deeds will hit the light so make no mistake about it, the time of exposure is coming so we had better be ready (Ephesians 5:8-14).

The days of telling right from wrong are long gone in this world that has become shrouded in the darkness by the Prince of Persia, Lucifer. We need to constantly put on our Belt of Truth and search for the light that guides us. Whoever follows the King will never walk in darkness (John 8:12). Putting on this belt will break the shackles of bondage that the enemy wrapped around your hands at birth. You will be able to slash through the lies in your marriage, your ministry, and your workplace with this belt sitting snugly around your waist.

Do *not* let the enemy trick your family into believing lies such as modern feminism where the woman is taught to usurp the role of the man as leader of the home. This lie puts woman over man and Satan over woman. The Belt of Truth will shine through, showing the true order that God intended of the woman over the kids, the man over the woman, and God over all. You are in charge of your household men. You wouldn't let anyone break in and harm your family in the physical realm so why let it happen in the spiritual? Make a good example of The Warrior-Priest for your children and speak God's truths out loud, teach them to your family, and burn them into the very core of your heart. Speaking of protecting and defending our families, let us move on to our next section on protecting and defending the weak!

CHAP†ER 25
PR⊕†EC†ING AND DEFENDING THE WEAK

*Defend the poor and fatherless: do justice to the afflicted
and needy. - Psalm 82.3*

Knights are sworn to protect women and defend the weak. All throughout classical literature and modern films we see the archetypical knight rescuing orphans from a burning church or saving a damsel in distress from an evil fire-breathing dragon. The Knights in Yahweh's army are sworn to do the same and we find evidence of this in many different verses. We also find many verses about defending ourselves, protecting our family, and fending off thieves or would be murderers. It is our God-given right to do these things and anyone that tells you different may not be examining the scriptures close enough.

If Father God gave you a gift or talent, He intends you to put that gift to use for His Kingdom. James 1:17 tells us that every good and perfect gift is given from the Father of Heavenly Lights. That means that if we are skilled or gifted in an area, assuming it isn't a sinful area, it is a gift from God. This makes it easy to eliminate any feeling of pride because we can identify the source. Even if you were to say "Well I put in all those hours of practice so it is from my own work.", I would ask you, "Who gave you the hands to craft, the brain to decipher, or the breath in your lungs to even be alive his day?" You can see that there is nothing we can do that He didn't already provide the means for.

Now, Ephesians 2:10 tells us that we are God's handiwork, created in Christ Jesus to do good works. It also tells us that those good works were prepared *in advance* by God for us to do. Exodus 35:10 when speaking of the building of the tabernacle asked for all who were skilled among God's people to come and make everything The Lord has commanded.

Lastly, Proverbs 22:29 informs us that if you see someone skilled in their work that they will serve before kings. We can now create a bigger picture given these three verses: We are the craftsmanship of Yahweh, given special skills and gifts to do tasks that He has already prepared for us to do for the betterment of His Kingdom, and if we do them well enough, we may even do them before kings!

> For we are his workmanship, created in Christ Jesus unto good works, which God hath before ordained that we should walk in them. - Ephesians 2:10

> Every good gift and every perfect gift is from above, and cometh down from the Father of lights, with whom is no variableness, neither shadow of turning. - James 1:17

I say all of this to say this one point. If God gave you strength, He intends you to *use it for His Kingdom*! This obviously applies to things other than strength but when it comes to defending the weak, He gave you strength so you can *defend*. In other cases, He gave you intelligence so you can *teach*. See where I'm going with this?

We then that are strong ought to bear the infirmities
of the weak, and not to please ourselves. Romans 15:1

If you have intelligence, you can use that to teach His people and
defend them in a court of law or just amongst other brethren. If you
have exceptional strength and an armed bandit is assaulting a man,
I would say it is your duty to defend him. This definitely does not
mean get involved in any and every situation. Proverbs 26:17 warns
us against getting involved in other people's problems that are not our
own. It likens it to grabbing a vicious dog by its ears!

He that passeth by, and meddleth with strife belonging
not to him, is like one that taketh a dog by the ears. -
Proverbs 26:17

So, where does that leave us? We need to use our free will to exercise
good discernment and Godly judgment. We know that Father gives
wisdom freely to those who ask (James 1:5) and it is His wisdom that
we can apply to our own discernment and judgments. When we have
repented of our sins and have practice hearing The Lord's voice, we
can then trust the Holy Spirit to give us the correct way to handle
things. We should think of the things His word has taught us then
listen for any "checks in the Spirit" when moving forward. Remember,
any "checks in the Spirit" will *always* line up with God's word and if
it doesn't then it is a different spirit you are hearing from. Take heed!
Not all spirits are good and if they cannot pass the test of confessing
that Jesus Christ is the son of God who came in the flesh then you are
dealing with the enemy!

Let us choose to use judgment (**discernment**): let
us know among ourselves what is good. - Job 34:4
(commentary added)

Teach me good judgment **(discernment)** and knowledge: for I have believed thy commandments. - Psalm 119:66 (commentary added)

Beloved, **believe not every spirit, but try the spirits whether they are of God**: because many false prophets are gone out into the world. Hereby know ye the Spirit of God: **Every spirit that confesseth that Jesus Christ is come in the flesh is of God: And every spirit that confesseth not that Jesus Christ is come in the flesh is not of God**: and this is that spirit of antichrist, whereof ye have heard that it should come; and even now already is it in the world. - 1 John 4:1-4 (emphasis added)

We know that Jesus said the greatest commandment is to love Him with all we have and to love our neighbors as ourselves (Matthew 22:36-40) and letting someone get beaten to death so you can "stay out of other's business" would be total neglect of loving your neighbor. I would use discernment and ask myself "Is staying out of this conflict going against a greater commandment than getting involved would be?" The only thing needed for evil to prosper is for good men to sit by and do nothing! Many people don't want to get involved out of sheer laziness whether it be not wanting to go through the hassle of breaking up a fight or not wanting to deal with talking to a police officer about what happened and taking time out of their precious day. Others refuse to do so out of self-preservation. Now if you have children, I am not saying to break up every fight you see and risk your life potentially leaving your wife and children to fend for themselves. We know what 1 Timothy has to say about people who don't provide for their families as being worse than unbelievers.

But if any provide not for his own, and especially for those of his own house, he hath denied the faith, and is worse than an infidel. 1 Timothy 5:8

I will, however, for certain circumstances, ask you this; what good is preserving your own life if you have already supposedly given that life over to Yahweh? Are we not called to *not* love our lives unto death? Are we not called to be a living sacrifice? Maybe this can change how you may view certain situations and self-preservation knowing that you have already given your earthly life to God in exchange for an eternity with Him.

> For whosoever will save his life shall lose it: and whosoever will lose his life for my sake shall find it. - Matthew 16:25

Proverbs 25:26 also sheds some light on what it is like when a righteous man steps aside to let wickedness through. It is the *duty* of the believer to expose and undo the unfruitful works of darkness (Ephesians 5:11). A knight stands when he is called to action. He uses discernment from The Lord to address how to handle every specific situation. Some call for restraint others call for action. Either way he tries to honor God and walk out His ways while approaching every dilemma life brings with a heart set on God's commands.

> Like a muddied spring or a polluted fountain is a righteous man who gives way before the wicked. - Proverbs 25:26 ESV

> And have no fellowship with the unfruitful works of darkness, but rather reprove them. - Ephesians 5:11

CHAP✝ER 26
SELF DEFENSE VS. REVENGE

*When a strong man armed keepeth his palace, his goods
are in peace - Luke 11:21*

A Knight of Yahweh is called to deliver the poor and needy from
the hand of the wicked (Psalm 82:4) and rescue the captives
condemned to death (Proverbs 24:11). The Lord expects us to
fight. He trains our hands for battle and strengthens our arms to draw
a bronze bow. I will start off by saying our greatest commandment
involves the loving of others so whenever possible, this should be our
main objective. However, sometimes our enemies do not allow for us
to sit back and do nothing and that is where we began our discussion.

Blessed be the Lord my strength which teacheth my
hands to war, and my fingers to fight. - Psalm 144:1

If He expects us to fight then we must fight by His rules. Jesus even told His disciples to sell their cloak and buy a sword if they didn't already have one when they were to go out and preach the gospel. That doesn't sound like the hippie messiah being preached by the feel-good church now does it? Let's take a closer look.

> And he said unto them, When I sent you without purse, and scrip, and shoes, lacked ye anything? And they said, Nothing. Then said he unto them, But now, he that hath a purse, let him take it, and likewise his scrip: and **he that hath no sword, let him sell his garment, and buy one**. For I say unto you, that this that is written must yet be accomplished in me, And he was reckoned among the transgressors: for the things concerning me have an end. **And they said, Lord, behold, here are two swords. And he said unto them, It is enough**. And he came out, and went, as he was wont, to the mount of Olives; and his disciples also followed him. - Luke 22:35-39 (emphasis added)

This is a fallen world and unfortunately death has reared its ugly head. We live in a dangerous place and mean sharks eat cute little seals every day. Then the cycle repeats. However, not every situation calls for action and we see an example of this when Peter drew his sword to stop the men from taking Jesus into custody. The Lord stopped him because Peter was unknowingly using violence and trying to stop a plan that was ordained by The Lord (Matthew 26:2). Jesus told him that if you live by the sword you die by the sword. Self-defense is not an excuse to live a violent life. It is important to use good discernment to make sure any decision we make is in line with our Father's will. Never forget that life is precious and we are all made in the image of God.

The fact of the matter is that we *will* encounter trouble in our times and The Lord wants us to be prepared. Moses told his people to arm themselves for war against the Midianites in Numbers 31:3. Luke 11:21 and Mark 3:27 speaks of a strong man being fully armed guarding his own mansions. It says that with him standing guard that all his belongings are safe and that no man can spoil a strong man's goods unless they first bind the strong man guarding them. Isaiah 49:24 asks "who can snatch the plunder from the hands of a warrior". The list goes on and on but one example that I hold very highly is the commands that came straight from Father God Himself. In Exodus 22:2-3 God was giving laws to Moses so he could take them back to His people and show them how to live. This is what He said.

> **If a thief is caught in the act of breaking in, and he is beaten to death, no one is guilty of bloodshed**. But if this happens after sunrise, there is guilt of bloodshed. A thief must make full restitution. If he is unable, he is to be sold because of his theft. - Exodus 22:2-3 HCSB (emphasis added)

God Himself said that if a thief is caught breaking at night and he is beaten to death *no one* is guilty of bloodshed! This is proof right here that we are able to defend ourselves. Jesus also told his disciples to buy swords so now we have an Old Testament and New Testament backing for where we are heading. What this verse in Exodus also shows us is that if it were day time then there would, in fact, be bloodguilt. What this shows is that Yahweh understands the scary and uncertain situations the darkness can add to a life or death situation. If it were day time it is assumed that it would be easier to manage and an element of secrecy would be eliminated for being able to see the culprit and the crime clearly. You would then be able to identify the thief and alert the law enforcement in your area.

I have had some friends interpret this verse to instead mean you are allowed to defend yourself but if you find the thief after the fact or away from your house then you are not able to kill them without guilt. I agree that we are not to avenge the theft after the fact because it would no longer fall under self-defense but rather under revenge. However, I do think that there is something to be said about the verse mentioning the sunrise and the theft as the same occasion. If you were to find a man in your house during the day you would be able to defend yourself but to go as far as killing him over theft would incur bloodguilt. You will have to delve deeper into this verse and decide for yourself.

The verse then moves on to say if the thief was caught alive, he would have to pay in full or work off the amount he stole through servitude. This shows that God is not only *merciful* but also *just*. This is another hidden dichotomy of our Lord. The mercy to forgive His children of all their sin and the justice to never let the unrepentant wicked go unpunished. He is merciful to forgive the repentant and just to punish the wicked...He is Yahweh Elohim.

After the flood we see Yahweh telling Noah and a small group of people, "whoever sheds the blood of a man, by man shall His blood be shed" (Genesis 9:6). Yahweh instituted the death penalty for murder among other crimes; however, the same is not to be said for killing in a wartime setting. This applies to the individual and to the group. Another important example of self-defense is in the book of Nehemiah. Nehemiah was led by God to rebuild the city walls. When his builders were doing their work, they began to be attacked by people opposing the construction of the walls. What did Nehemiah do? Sit on his hands and love his neighbor as they killed his builders? Nope! He posted guards and told the builders to start bringing their swords to work (Nehemiah 4:16-18). They had building materials in one hand and a sword in the other and guess what...the walls got built!

There are some cases in scripture where believers of Yahweh are martyred or killed for their faith. This is shown when Yahweh has specifically put that calling on a man or woman's life and is by no means the norm. Unless Father is calling you to be a martyr within a shadow of a doubt then you are to protect those around you and even yourself.

Now before we go any further it's time to address some seemingly inconsistent things in the Word. Now we *know* there are no contradictions in the Bible but many have trouble justifying a God who in the book of Joshua tells Joshua and his men to kill all the men women and children but who also says thou shalt not kill. Yeshua tells us to love our neighbor then other places in the Bible warriors are being praised for their war exploits! What do we do with this? Research, that's what! Let us lay the first foundation before we start our study. God can do whatever He wants with any of His vessels whether it be destroying them or lifting them up. It is not up to the pot to question the doings of the potter.

> But in a great house there are not only vessels of gold and of silver, but also of wood and of earth; and some to honour, and some to dishonour. 2 Timothy 2:20

> Hath not the potter power over the clay, of the same lump to make one vessel unto honour, and another unto dishonour? - Romans 9:21

Once we lay that groundwork, we can get into who Joshua was destroying. Many of the people Joshua was told to destroy were from *known* clans of GIANTS! Amorites, Canaanites, Anakites, and many other giant clans were all running rampant throughout the Promised Land. In case you are unaware there is a seed war that has been raging since the dawn of time between the seed of Adam and the seed of the serpent. There is the bloodline of Adam and the bloodlines of the Nephilim. For more on this whole topic, I recommend checking out the work of guys like Michael Heiser, Derek Gilbert, Steve Quayle, L.A. Marzulli, and Gary Wayne to name a few. That is a discussion for another book.

So, God can do what He chooses with His creation and the purpose of Joshua's conquest was to wipe out the last remaining Nephilim clans and those who have interbred and allied themselves with them. Great! Now we get to the word study. When Yahweh said "thou shalt not kill" the word He used for "kill" was "*Ratsach*". This word "*Ratsach*" is never used in conjunction with war. It is used to describe murder and usually in an unlawful way resulting in bloodguilt before God. Yahweh is very clear that we are not to shed *innocent* blood which would be a great disrespect. We would be destroying something made in His royal image. Human life is precious and killing should NEVER be taken lightly. Taking a life changes you forever and the memories of such may never leave. You might always remember every detail about the time where you took a life. It is nasty business even in cases of self-defense and this is why these distinctions can be so important.

Ratzah / Ratsach - Never used in conjunction with war.
Phonetic Spelling: (raw-tsakh')
Definition: to murder, slay

When Yahweh was telling His people to fight in war and slay their enemies, He used the word "*Harag*". "*Harag*" means killing or slaying and it's usually used when talking about war. So "thou shalt not kill" is different from killing in war times. Thou shalt not murder would be closer to the Hebrew meaning.

Harag
Phonetic Spelling: (haw-rag')
Definition: to kill, slay

War is not murder. God wouldn't tell you to not kill and then tell you it was okay to kill an intruder. He makes a critical distinction between the two. An exception is also made when talking about legitimate self-defense and from our look into Exodus we saw that a man defended his home and did *not* incur bloodguilt. That pretty much settles the case in my mind and if anyone tries to tell you that you cannot defend you or your family from intruders or would-be murderers you can tell them "Thanks, but no thanks! I wouldn't want to be considered less than an unbeliever in the Kingdom of God!"

But if any provide not for his own, and especially for those of his own house, he hath denied the faith, and is worse than an infidel. - 1 Timothy 5:8

Now since you have all made it this far in our noble quest, I shall grant you a bonus word! "*Cherem/Kherem*" was term that God used at times when telling Joshua to clear out the giant clans or other groups of particularly nasty people or their belongings. It basically means to be "devoted to destruction" or "put under the ban". What it means is to wipe these people out and leave nothing behind. Pretty intense!

Cherem/Kherem
Phonetic Spelling: (khay'-rem)
Definition: devoted thing, devotion, ban

REVENGE

We are now beginning to understand the Code of Chivalry The Lord has given us for battle and self-defense, a code of ethics if you will. We know that He forbids murder, He allows self-defense, and wants us to protect the weak. He tells Peter to not "live by the sword" or lead a lifestyle of violence. What are some of the other "battle ethics" He gives us? I can tell you one more thing He strictly forbids. Revenge.

> Dearly beloved, avenge not yourselves, but rather give place unto wrath: for it is written, Vengeance is mine; I will repay, saith the Lord. - Romans 12:19

> Say not, I will do so to him as he hath done to me: I will render to the man according to his work. - Proverbs 24:29

God hates us taking revenge. Revenge, much like pride, elevates us to the place of supreme judge and jury. It assumes that we know what is best and how to dole out what one may deserve. This is usurping the position of our Father who is Himself the supreme judge. We have a very limited view of situations but God has a bird's eye view. He sees and knows all and not only that but He is the only one who is morally capable of judging someone's fate. Only a perfect God can make a perfect moral code to judge by. Do not try to take His place. You will one day have to give an account for all your actions so the sooner you deal with these issues the better (Matthew 16:27).

Revenge not only facilitates pride but it also goes against loving our neighbor. Self-defense would be protecting one's self or others to fend off an attacker whereas revenge would be not stopping at the point of self-defense. It would be taking things further. When we do this, we are going out of the boundaries The Lord has set for our self-defense.

Jesus told His people a greater commandment than the one they had previously heard when He said, "an eye for an eye" is to be replaced with "turning the other cheek."

> Ye have heard that it hath been said, An eye for an eye, and a tooth for a tooth: But I say unto you, That ye resist not evil: but whosoever shall smite thee on thy right cheek, turn to him the other also. - Matthew 5:38-39

This did not mean you were no longer allowed to defend yourself. What this meant was that in cases where you no longer needed to defend yourself or others you now had a limit of how far you could go. If someone walked up to you and slapped you across the face and walked off and you decided to chase them down and slap them back then you have crossed into the "eye for an eye" territory which Jesus warns against. We are to avoid trouble where we can and to remain at peace with all men. He wishes for us to not repay evil for evil but to love our neighbor as ourselves and to leave the vengeance to Him.

> Recompense to no man evil for evil. Provide things honest in the sight of all men. If it be possible, as much as lieth in you, live peaceably with all men. Dearly beloved, avenge not yourselves, but rather give place unto wrath: for it is written, **Vengeance is mine; I will repay, saith the Lord.** - Romans 12:17-19 (emphasis added)

The goal is not to justify the harming of your neighbor but to make clear some of the boundaries that Yeshua has set for us when protecting those we love. We are called to live peaceably with all men as much as we can and to love our neighbor as ourselves. If it physically hurts your or your family and is a threat, defend. If it hurts your pride, move on. While you are walking away from a situation there is no reason why you can't walk away in style right? Well if you are going to walk away in style, you will need some new boots… Boots of Peace!

THE BOOTS OF PEACE

And your feet shod with the preparation of the gospel of peace - Ephesians 6:15

You have finally uncovered the last piece of your Armor of God set. It has been a long adventurous journey and your quest for the armor is completed. You have fortified your head with the knowledge of God's kingdom from your Helmet of Salvation. You have protected your body from the fiery darts of the enemy with your Shield of Faith. You have guarded your heart against uncleanness and sin with your Breastplate of Righteousness. You have girded your loins with the Belt of Truth. At last, you must also cover your feet with the calming gospel of peace given by The Boots of Peace.

Now that you know how to deal with revenge and have a new heart set on living peaceably with all men, you can receive your next piece of the Armor of God battle set...The Boots of Peace.

At the time when Paul wrote Ephesians one of the great warriors of the day was the Roman Legionnaires. They wore what was called a "*Caliga*" and it was a cross between a laced sandal and a sturdy boot. The bottom had a thick leather sole and was studded with nails for better traction. This is the sandal Paul most likely wrote about but since we are all knights here can we at least go ahead and picture some really cool metal plated boots or at the very least some fancy leather slippers? Perfect. Moving on...

The Hebrew word for peace is "*shalom*" and it is defined as completeness, soundness, welfare, or peace. The verse in Ephesians we are looking at tells us to have our feet "shod with the preparation of the gospel of peace." In other words, we need to have our feet covered with the good news of completeness, soundness, welfare, and peace. This can be viewed as having every step we take covered in God's good news of peace and soundness of mind. This directly relates to how we deal with other people as well as ourselves. Since we know we are called to live peaceably with our fellow man as much as we can, the understanding of this piece of armor is crucial for The Warrior-Priest.

Transliteration: **Shalom**
Phonetic Spelling: (shaw-lome')
Definition: completeness, soundness, welfare, peace

Satan and his dark allies will seek to rob you of your peace and destroy your relationships with others in any way they can. They hate peace and wish to replace it with destruction and disorder. They wish for you to draw out every wrong done to you, hold long-lasting grudges, and to walk around too proud to forgive or reconcile. He wants to plant what Hebrews 12:15 calls a "root of bitterness" inside you and have it grow and grow until the roots wrap around you and strangle any chance you have of forgiveness and happiness.

> Looking diligently lest any man fail of the grace of God;
> lest any root of bitterness springing up trouble you, and
> thereby many be defiled - Hebrews 12:15

Many things can steal your peace with others or yourself. Most commonly wounds from childhood or any traumatic experience, among other things, in life can sow a deep root of bitterness early on. The pain from our past can keep hurting us well into the future if it is not prayed over and left at the feet of Yeshua so He can pick up our burdens and carry them because He cares for us (1 Peter 5:7). We must not be easily offended or quick to anger. A man who has no control over his spirit is like a castle with no walls (Proverbs 25:28). Some people suffer from abandonment issues or being cheated on as an adult and have yet to let go of the pain. Remember this, not learning to let our pain go is like a serpent who is coiled around a dagger. The serpent holds on to the dagger tighter and tighter not realizing that it is only cutting itself deeper and deeper. We need to let the pain go, forgive anyone at fault and lay hold of the peace that our Father offers us freely.

Our peace is directly tied to our health and if we don't have peace with ourselves and others then we will ultimately never be as healthy as we should be. The sooner we realize that we are complete with God and need no one's approval or acceptance the sooner we can start to have interpersonal peace. It is a combination of being complete in Jesus Christ and clearing out your spiritual house from all pain, trauma, broken trust, and betrayal. If we are called to love our neighbor as ourselves then we must first be able to love ourselves. After we have forgiven even ourselves, we can then repair and maybe even reconcile with those who have wronged us or who we have wronged. This does not mean you have to rekindle toxic relationships; heaven forbid! For those who we cannot reconcile with due to toxicity we can at the very least stop letting their actions affect us and release them from the debt we feel they owe us for hurting us. We do for them what Yeshua does for us, which is wiping the sin from our accounts. If we are dead to self then what are we doing worrying about how the world treats us? The world hated our Father so why should it treat us any better (John 15:18)? Did Jesus go around feeling sorry for Himself or did He move on and still maintain His peace? He maintained His peace and He is the standard by which we try to walk out. This isn't to minimize your pain but, on the contrary, to release you from bondage to it. Let go of the blade cutting your hand and start to heal.

The fact of the matter is that you cannot go on as an effective believer in this world if you never have peace. You will have an existence of servitude to a cruel master where not even your own mind provides escape. It won't be long before you seek escape in drugs, alcohol, and sex, all of which will amplify your pain and endanger your eternal soul. If we were once enemies of God and He forgave us then we are to do the same for our enemies. Colossians 3:12-15 speaks about having compassion, kindness, humility, gentleness, patience, forgiveness, and to live in unity which the peace of Jesus Christ rules in our heart. Doesn't that just sound peaceful to hear? Imagine how it feels put into practice. This is a daily battle to maintain your peace and it should never be left sitting. Satan and his minions *hate* the unity of believers and he seeks to create division wherever he can. Why do you think there are so many different Christian denominations? Together we are strong and that is the last thing the enemy wants, a united front. Love is what binds the believers together and peace is our defense against the chaos of evil.

We must use the metal studs on the bottom of The Boots of Peace and dig them into the ground, side by side with our brothers and sisters in The Lord and REFUSE to give any ground to those foul knaves in the enemy's camp! The Boots of Peace allow us to stand strong and to be courageous as we unite together in love as our Commander tells us to. The body of Christ must function together as a whole. Unfortunately, people will always let you down given enough time just as you have let many down yourself. You will still be hurt and still get angry but you are not to let it cause you to sin or to even let the sun go down on that anger lest you give the devil a perfect opening to assault you and steal your peace (Ephesians 4:26-27).

When we are wronged Matthew 18:15-16 tells us to go to the person alone to handle it and give them a chance to fix it or to explain. If that doesn't work, we bring a trustworthy friend with us and confront them in hopes of an unbiased witness able to provide a case. Lastly, we involve the church and if that doesn't work, we let them go and treat them as an unbeliever. This doesn't mean disrespect them it just means to cut them loose. After that process is complete, we are free of the burden and must *choose* to stop being angry or hurt. We essentially give the rights to our negative emotion over to our loving Father and let Him sort it out while we regain our Boots of Peace. We are to love our enemies and pray for those who persecute us (Matthew 5:44).

> But I say to you, love your enemies, bless those who curse you, do good to those who hate you, and pray for those who spitefully use you and persecute you - Matthew 5:44

It shouldn't be hard to make a habit of forgiving because we all have sinned and fall short of the glory of God (Romans 3:23) and we are told that we will be forgiven with the same measure that we forgive (Matthew 6:14-15). You would want to be cut slack when you mess up right? So would other people. Ask the Holy Spirit to reveal times or events in your life that traumatized you, left you with a lasting wound, or continue to steal your peace. Forgive any who you remember have wronged you and leave the burden with your Father. Remember, no one is perfect except the Father who would never let us down and we cannot waste time for the days are evil and our time is short (Ephesians 5:16) ...too short to not equip The Boots of Peace and walk daily in the freedom they provide through our Savior Christ Jesus.

⊕BEYING ΠAN'S LAW

Another one of Yeshua's laws of chivalry is the obeying of man's law unless it contradicts His law. Let us look at Romans 13:1-7 piece by piece to see what God says about our intended approach to obedience to the law.

> Let every soul be subject unto the higher powers. For there is no power but of God: the powers that be are ordained of God. - Romans 13:1

We see that He intends for every one of us to be subject to the higher powers. He says that there is no power higher than Him and that He is the one who ordains people in a position of power.

> Whosoever therefore resisteth the power, resisteth the ordinance of God: and they that resist shall receive to themselves damnation. - Romans 13:2

Here we see that whoever resists the power that God has ordained is, in turn, resisting God Himself and shall receive damnation! Yikes, that doesn't sound too good.

> For rulers are not a terror to good works, but to the evil. Wilt thou then not be afraid of the power? Do that which is good, and thou shalt have praise of the same: - Romans 13:3

The Lord says that good rulers are not a problem for good people and only provide a problem for evil people. Do good and you shouldn't have an issue with a good ruler.

For he is the minister of God to thee for good. But if thou do that which is evil, be afraid; for he beareth not the sword in vain: for he is the minister of God, a revenger to execute wrath upon him that doeth evil. Wherefore ye must needs be subject, not only for wrath, but also for conscience sake. For this cause pay ye tribute also: for they are God's ministers, attending continually upon this very thing. - Romans 13:4-6

Now He says that a good ruler is put in place to do good for everyone. He says that if your people are evil then be afraid because He does not draw His sword unless He tends to use it! He says an evil ruler is a judgment on an evil people to recompense them for their unrighteous deeds. So, you will be subject to these evil men not only as a punishment but also to clear your conscience. You will be paying tribute to them because they are God's ministers doing His appointed work.

Render therefore to all their dues: tribute to whom tribute is due; custom to whom custom; fear to whom fear; honour to whom honour. - Romans 13:7

Lastly, we are told to pay them what they are due whether it be money, customs, fear, or honor. It is very clear that we are to obey man's law. The *only* condition where you are allowed to go against man's law is if it goes against God's law because Yahweh is the higher authority as seen in Acts 5:29.

Then Peter and the other apostles answered and said,
We ought to obey God rather than men. - Acts 5:29

CHAP✝ER 27
DAMSEL IN DIS✝RESS

*Likewise, ye husbands, dwell with them according to
knowledge, giving honour unto the wife, as unto the
weaker vessel, and as being heirs together of the grace of
life; that your prayers be not hindered. - 1 Peter 3:7*

When speaking about defending the weak and being a righteous protector there is one more area that we need to touch on. For our last topic, I wanted to address something that is the main part of the Code of Chivalry and also of equal importance in God's law. Something that is essential to the core beliefs and personality of a true knight. That topic would be respecting women. It is the duty of every knight to have the utmost respect towards women who are in fact the weaker vessel. If you are a woman take no offense! The weaker vessel does not mean lesser in value or importance.

Women can make some of the fiercest warriors of all. I believe Father designed a specific role for each gender but both genders overlap in many ways. Man is called to be a protector however a woman can protect as well. A good woman can be your armor bearer in battle. The flesh of your flesh fighting side by side with you. However, when it comes time to sacrifice, the man should be in the line of fire shielding the woman and children from harm while he takes the brunt of it upon his Shield of Faith. The hierarchy that God intended has Yahweh at the head of the marriage, then the man is the head of the house and then the woman is head of the children. I believe a man should be working and providing enough for a woman to stay home and homeschool the kids. This would take them out of the grubby mitts of the public-school system and replace it with a strong woman of God to influence their lives. For the man, he should work to provide then come home and start his second shift of the day that entails catering to his wife and spending time with the children. His day ends when he hits the pillow and he does not mentally check out a moment before. The main trait of good leadership is the ability to be a servant. Jesus modeled that better than anyone and while a man may be the leader this in no way should enable him to lord this fact over his wife. If he is doing it right then he is serving her with his leadership. Weaker vessel or not we are all one in Christ Jesus.

> There is neither Jew nor Greek, there is neither bond nor free, there is neither male nor female: for ye are all one in Christ Jesus. - Galatians 3:28

> Nevertheless neither is the man without the woman, neither the woman without the man, in the Lord. - 1 Corinthians 11:11

When you get married you become one flesh and it is important that you choose your partner based on biblical principles alone. If you read Proverbs 31 and the woman you are interested in sounds nothing like that I would suggest moving on. Pray and seek The Lord's face when finding a partner and just remember beauty fades and someone who is not on fire for The Lord will only bring your walk down. When

I chose my wife, I looked for fear of The Lord first, then kindness, then intelligence. Without fear of The Lord, you shouldn't even be considering the person as a companion. Kindness and intelligence, I chose because if I am going to spend the better part of my life with someone, they had better have a kind heart and wisdom from The Lord. The fact that my wife is beautiful as well is just a delightful bonus (I love you, Bri)!

Now God commands husbands to love their wife in the same way that He loves the church and for wives to be subject to their husbands and if you choose a disobedient wife or a wife that disrespects her parents then you are in for it, pal. Also, if you aren't holding up your end of the bargain then you are in just as big of a mess. God designed things a certain way for a good reason...because it works!

> Likewise, ye wives, be in subjection to your own husbands; that, if any obey not the word, they also may without the word be won by the conversation of the wives; - 1 Peter 3:1

Women should be respected as the weaker vessel and what that means is be sensitive to their feelings. They don't need to be coddled but you can no longer be a single brute walking through life like a bull in a china shop. You must cater to her feelings and needs while never coming off as condescending or prideful. You are nothing without half your flesh so don't let pride creep in and mess this whole thing up. Women are strong and will fight by your side to the very end if you pick the right one. Treat them with the respect they deserve. Do not be inappropriate around them, crude, or vulgar. We shouldn't act that way anyway but especially in front of a woman. Another thing to avoid is roughhousing. Physical strength against a weaker vessel is a recipe for injury or if it gets nasty even jail time. Don't treat her like one of the guys because she is not one of your guy friends. She is the best friend you will ever have in your life. So, give her the proper respect she deserves as your sister in arms waging war on the enemy into eternity!

> She girdeth her loins with strength, and strengtheneth her arms. - Proverbs 31:17

> Strength and honour are her clothing; and she shall
> rejoice in time to come. - Proverbs 31:25

Protect them with your life and never cross the boundaries of dishonoring them with your words or actions. Remember they are women and not men, yet do not baby them. They are big girls and women warriors of God. Pray with them every day, seek their guidance and keep them involved in the plans you make. They are your most trusted advisor apart from God and by far the greatest gift you will ever receive while on this earth, apart from salvation.

VIC+⊕RY RES+S WI+H THE L⊕RD

As we come to the end of our self-defense and protecting the weak discussion, I wish to leave you with one final conclusion on the matter. We can train endless hours, be master preppers storing up years of supplies, or have the most state-of-the-art defense technology and weaponry but without The Lord, it is all for naught. It is only in His name that we can push back our enemies or trample our foes (Psalm 44:5-7). Trust not in the sword or gun to bring you victory or safety. In Proverbs 21:31 the Hebrew word used for safety is "*teshuah*". This word also means deliverance or salvation. It has also been translated as VICTORY.

> Transliteration: **Teshuah**
> Phonetic Spelling: (tesh-oo-aw')
> Definition: deliverance, salvation

Knowing what this word means I want you to keep that in mind as you read this next verse. Really think about everything we've gone over and then read this verse. Pray to Father God that this is burned into the heart of all His warrior-priests and for you personally as well.

> *The horse is prepared against the day of battle: but*
> *safety* (**victory**) *is of the Lord. - Proverbs 21:31*
> *(emphasis added)*

CONCLUSION:
A QUEST COMPLETED

But he that shall endure unto the end, the same shall be saved - Matthew 24:13

O ur journey together is at its end; however, your own personal journey through life with The Warrior-Priest Mindset has only just begun. We learned about the bravery of The Lion and the kind-hearted love of The Lamb. We learned about the courage of The Warrior and the holiness of The Priest. Finally, we learned about the perseverance and faith of The Knight. We have formed them all into one **Warrior-Priest Mindset** and along the way, we collected pieces to the set of the Armor of God. Remember that you can always be better today than you were yesterday if you never give up. Always strive to be the best version of yourself that you can and push others in love to do the same.

Now the time has come for the reward of completing your Warrior-Priest training. But first, you must equip your full set of the Armor of God and acquire the necessary upgrade to your armor. It is with great honor that we upgrade your Armor of God into the Armor of LIGHT!

> The night is far spent, the day is at hand: let us, therefore, cast off the works of darkness, and let us put on the armour of light. - Romans 13:12

Your armor is now infused with light from Heaven to aid you in your crusade against the darkness. Everything is now coming to a close yet something seems to be missing? I feel like we need a weapon...Of course! We have covered ourselves defensively but we have yet to cover ourselves *offensively*. This is where we are finally and truly knighted into **The Order of the Warrior-Priest**. Now kneel before God and accept your reward for the quest you have embarked on...The Sword of the Spirit!

THE SWORD OF THE SPIRIT

...And the sword of the Spirit, which is the word of God
– Ephesians 6:17

No knight is complete without his sword. As a member of The Order of The Warrior-Priest, your sword is not only physical but spiritual as well. It is the only offensive item from The Lord's Battle Gear that we receive. The Sword of the Spirit is, in fact, the Word of God. King Yeshua even returns as Messiah Ben David with a double-edged sword coming out of His mouth (Revelation 1:16) which is a very interesting image to behold! Since the Sword of the Spirit and the Word of God are one and the same, we must learn how to wield the Word of God as we would a sword.

APPLYING THE WORD AND WIELDING THE SWORD

To successfully wield the shining blade of the Spirit we must be able to effectively apply the Word of God to our lives. We are told to study the word to prove it true as the faithful Bereans did. We need to follow every bit of the Word without picking or choosing. God will have mercy with us as we learn but we are not to be lazy in this undertaking. He will render each man according to His deeds and He judges by the heart so do not be found wanting (Romans 2:6-8). The day is here where true worshippers worship the Father in spirit and in truth and we have His grace to begin to do the same (John 4:23-24). Walk out everything that you learned, read, heard, or have seen Jesus do so you can ensure that the Lord of Peace shall be with you (Philippians 4:9). We only deceive ourselves if we read the Word but cannot do the word like a man who knows everything about swords except how to use one (James 1:22).

> These were more noble than those in Thessalonica, in that they received the word with all readiness of mind, and searched the scriptures daily, whether those things were so. - Acts 17:11

Grab hold of the hilt of this powerful sword and pray in the Spirit as you wield it. Your safety rests in the Father and He frees you from fear to fight without looking back. For anyone who wields the blade then turns back from it is not fit to fight for the King.

> And Jesus said unto him, No man, having put his hand to the plough, and looking back, is fit for the kingdom of God. - Luke 9:62

The five pieces of your Armor of Light are made to defend against man and demon alike; however, you only have one weapon to attack with. This should show us that we are to defend more than we are to attack. That is not to say that we will never lay down holy fire upon the brow of a demon but most of the time we are the shield in the night protecting others from the fiery darts. Cast out demons, heal the sick, and grow in faith as you apply the Word of God to every aspect of your life. If anyone tells you anything, first, test it against the Word of God and ALWAYS take it to The Lord in prayer. He is the only reliable person you can trust. We have angels disguising themselves as the pagan gods of this world, we have disembodied spirits of the Nephilim giants posing as dead relatives, and we have our own fellow man warring with us as serpents bruise our heels. This life is not an easy one but it is the only one The Warrior-Priest can walk.

Your sword will heal, kill, and defend as long as you keep your relationship with the Father your main priority. The armor and the sword will not be effective without the one who made them empowering them to keep you safe and make you strong. Finally, brothers and sisters, **be STRONG AND COURAGEOUS for THE LORD thy God is with you WHEREVER you go!** Now get out there and FIGHT!

Be strong and of a good courage; be not afraid,
neither be thou dismayed: for the Lord thy God is
with thee whithersoever thou goest.
Joshua 1:9

REFERENCES

Hebrew Words

"Ratzah/Ratsach" Biblestudytools.com,
https://www.biblestudytools.com/lexicons/hebrew/kjv/ratsach.html

"Yare'/Yirah" Biblestudytools.com,
https://www.biblestudytools.com/lexicons/hebrew/kjv/yare-2.html

"Kohen/Kahan" Biblestudytools.com,
https://www.biblestudytools.com/lexicons/hebrew/kjv/kohen.html

"Cherem/Kherem" Biblestudytools.com,
https://www.biblestudytools.com/lexicons/hebrew/kjv/cherem.html

"Harag" Biblestudytools.com,
https://www.biblestudytools.com/lexicons/hebrew/kjv/harag.html

"Komer" Biblehub.com,
https://biblehub.com/hebrew/3649.htm

"Shalom" Biblehub.com,
https://biblehub.com/str/hebrew/7965.htm

"Teshuah" Biblehub.com,
https://biblehub.com/str/hebrew/8668.htm

"Mashiach" Biblehub.com,
https://biblehub.com/str/hebrew/4899.htm

Greek Words

"Nous" Biblestudytools.com,
https://www.biblestudytools.com/lexicons/greek/kjv/nous.html

"Phobeo/Phobos" Biblestudytools.com,
https://www.biblestudytools.com/lexicons/greek/kjv/phobeo.html

"Diamonizomai" Biblehub.com,
https://biblehub.com/greek/1139.htm

"Hiereus" Biblehub.com,
https://biblehub.com/str/greek/2409.htm

"Thorax" Biblehub.com,
https://biblehub.com/str/greek/2382.htm

"Dikaikosune" Biblehub.com,
https://biblehub.com/greek/1343.htm

"Metaschématizó" Biblehub.com,
https://biblehub.com/greek/3345.htm

Latin Words

"Scutum" Latin-dictionary.net,
https://latin-dictionary.net/definition/34414/scutum-scuti

"Caliga" Latin-dictionary.net,
https://latin-dictionary.net/search/latin/caliga

English Words

"Perspective" Lexico.com,
https://www.lexico.com/en/definition/perspective

"Dichotomy" Lexico.com,
https://www.lexico.com/en/definition/dichotomy

"Meekness" Lexico.com,
https://www.lexico.com/en/definition/meekness

"Yoga" Lexico.com,
https://www.lexico.com/en/definition/yoga

"Hinduism" Lexico.com,
https://www.lexico.com/en/definition/hinduism

"Scoffer" Vocabulary.com,
https://www.vocabulary.com/dictionary/scoffer